Taxidermy Guide

Third Edition

Taxidermy Guide
Third Edition

Russell Tinsley

Stoeger Publishing Company

Stoeger Publishing.
Great Outdoor Books Since 1925

STOEGER PUBLISHING COMPANY
is a division of Benelli U.S.A.

Benelli U.S.A.
Vice President and General Manager: Stephen Otway
Director of Brand Marketing and Communications:
  Stephen McKelvain
Vice President of Sales/Strategic Marketing:
  Jack Muety

Stoeger Publishing Company
President: Jeffrey Reh
Publisher: Jay Langston
Managing Editor: Harris J. Andrews
Art Director: Cynthia T. Richardson
Imaging Specialist: William Graves
Publishing Assistant: Christine Lawton

Taxidermy Guide
Cover Design and Photograph: Ray Wells

© 1990, 1977, 1967 by Russell Tinsley
Fourth Printing, 2002

Published by Stoeger Publishing Company
17603 Indian Head HIghway, Suite 200
Accokeek, Maryland 20607

BK6444
ISBN:0-88317-156-2
Library of Congress Control Number: 76-54416
Manufactured in the United States of America

Distributed to the book trade and
to the sporting goods trade by:
Stoeger Industries
17603 Indian Head HIghway, Suite 200
Accokeek, Maryland 20607
301 283-6300 Fax: 301 283-6986
E-mail: info@stoegerindustries.com
Web Address: www.stoegerindustries.com

Contents

Introduction

Taxidermy Guide is now into its third decade, and this is the third revised edition. When I first collaborated with taxidermist Lem Rathbone in producing the original edition back in 1967, I had no inkling the book would be as popular as it has been, nor that it would have such staying power. But really, upon reflection, it is not surprising. Taxidermy is within anyone's ability; it is a process that can be easily learned at home; and as a hobby, it's not all that expensive.

As I wrote in the introduction to the original edition, I had always been skeptical of how-to books, since most promised more than they delivered. And the instructions, when they were accurate, often proved to be complicated to the point of frustration. At Rathbone's suggestion, I decided to try a project myself to determine if taxidermy was indeed a practical home hobby. I had never tried taxidermy and figured that if old "ten thumbs" could do a reasonable mount job, anyone could.

Following Rathbone's written instructions, and after obtaining the necessary tools and materials, I began to cape a white-tailed deer and make a shoulder mount. Surprisingly, the finished product came out better than I had hoped. The job wasn't all that difficult, but it was time consuming; lacking experience, my pace was naturally slow.

But I did learn from my mistakes, and I decided to try another shoulder-mount job. This time, having shot photos of the process, I felt more comfortable with the procedure and entered into the project with far more confidence. That second mount hangs in my office today. It was the biggest buck I'd ever shot up to that time, more than 20 years ago, and it is still in excellent condition. The fact that I did the mounting myself makes this buck a little more special than other deer I've shot.

Yes, taxidermy can be learned from a book, and it can be very rewarding. I've received hundreds of testimonials about it over the years; in fact, the book has helped inspire some young hobbyists to consider taxidermy as a career. One of them is Chris Streetman, a partner in Cen-Tex Taxidermy Studios, located in Austin, Texas. Streetman remembers reading my book and getting interested in taxidermy when he was about 12 years old. Later, he served an apprenticeship with some established taxidermists before starting his own business.

Rathbone, knowing what it takes to succeed, has helped a lot of budding taxidermists like me. He began his own taxidermy business as a teenager himself, and by the time we collaborated on the original edition of this work he'd already had more than 40 years experience as a professional taxidermist. He's retired now, but he leaves behind a new generation of taxidermists, including Jimmy Bird, his stepson, who took over Lem's business and has helped considerably with this revision.

The methods used in various taxidermy projects that Rathbone first taught me are still in widespread use, but today's taxidermists have many more options. More materials are available from an ever growing number of supply houses. For example, there's a dry curing mix, sold as either Dry Preservative or Instant Preserve; there's also a preparation called "Liqua-Tan" for animal hides that eliminates the need for the pickling process. Nevertheless, I've kept the formula for the pickling solution (which preserves the hide and prevents the hair from falling out) in the Appendix because some taxidermists still prefer pickling over the new dry cure or commercial liquid methods.

Probably the biggest advancement of all since the second edition of *Taxidermy Guide* was published in 1977 is in the variety of forms (mannequins) now available for birds and fish, big-game shoulder mounts and even whole animals. The form or mannequin is the inside structure that gives a mount its basic lifelike appearance and makes it rigid. Such forms can be bought in the form of urethane, a semi-hard plastic. Rather than building each one by hand, these urethane forms can be mass-produced, enabling the taxidermist to produce more quality work in less time.

For the home hobbyist, of course, time is not always a major consideration. Consequently, you can stay with the traditional methods that have been the mainstays of taxidermy since before the turn of the century. At home, you can create a body for a bird mount using only paper excelsior and twine; you can carve a fish form out of wood instead of buying a urethane mannequin; or you can build a big-game shoulder mount mannequin from paper. This book will tell you how to do all these things.

There are still a few professional taxidermists around who prefer to do certain jobs the old-fashioned way. Chris Streetman uses both the old and the new, depending on the job. He likes the urethane forms for most birds and fish, but for big-game shoulder mounts he prefers the paper mannequins that he makes himself. "That way," he explains, "I have full control over the job and can build a mannequin that best represents the species involved. A Texas deer, or any other southern deer, for example, has characteristics that differ from the northern deer. But if I ordered a mannequin for a Texas deer, it will most likely have the shape and size of a northern deer. As a result, my finished mount won't look right."

While the fundamentals may remain the same, each taxidermist has his own methods, the ones that work best for him, year in and year out. As I wrote in my original introduction more than 20 years ago, you can't succeed in taxidermy without using your imagination and common sense. Even with the most basic job, you will run into problems that must be solved in a creative manner. There will come times when you've seemingly reached an impasse. When this happens, look at the problem objectively and think about it long and hard. The answer will almost always come to you in time.

There's one more thing: if you truly enjoy the challenge of taxidermy, you ought to think about making it a career. Many professionals, like Lem Rathbone and Chris Streetman, got interested in taxidermy as a hobby before they made it their profession. The possibilities in taxidermy are far-reaching, limited only by the extent of your initiative and imagination. Always remember that, and good luck in taxidermy.

Author Russell Tinsley

1/Beginning Taxidermy

1/Beginning Taxidermy

During his 50 years as a professional taxidermist, Lem Rathbone, now retired, enjoyed many interesting experiences. One that he is particularly fond of telling about concerns a time he was showing a woman his shop. While she was looking at the various wildlife mounts along the wall, she happened to brush her arm against a large owl. The bird was perched on a limb, wings outspread, as if poised to pounce upon its prey. The woman turned to see what she'd hit and came face to face with the sinister-looking owl. Instinctively, she jumped back in alarm. After realizing her mistake, she grinned sheepishly.

"That thing gave me a terrible fright," she admitted. "For a moment there I thought it was alive!"

This was the ultimate compliment for taxidermist Rathbone. In his profession, the craftsman strives to bring an animal or bird or fish back to "life" as realistically as is possible in an inanimate mount.

Webster's dictionary defines taxidermy as "the art of preparing, stuffing, etc., the skins of animals to make them appear lifelike." The two key words in this definition are "art" and "lifelike." Most people would not consider taxidermy an art, yet in many ways it is like realistic painting. The artist looks at a scene and tries to reproduce it with various shades of paint on canvas. The best paintings seem to come alive; they have a "feel" that someone looking at them can grasp; they have individual personalities.

The taxidermist takes an animal, bird or fish and tries to mount it so that it appears actually alive. This goes beyond technology. A mount of a bird, for instance, might be good technically, yet not seem "alive." The taxidermist strives for balance and personality in his work. The extent of his skill determines whether a mount seems artificial or startlingly realistic.

Obtaining a mount which is technically good and also has this lifelike quality is no accident. There is a personal challenge involved. This is what I like about taxidermy. It gives a person a chance to express himself. Yet in many ways taxidermy is like building a model. The taxidermist fits many varied pieces together until he obtains a finished product. Each progressive step requires skill and care. Thus taxidermy is an art, but it is also a craft. And, in addition, it is a hobby that anyone can pursue at home at very little expense.

Taxidermy has made much advancement in modern times. No one knows the exact date of its origin, but according to *World Book Encyclopedia,* "The art has reached its highest development during the last four centuries, although it was known for a long period before that."

Yet taxidermy has not really changed that much. The basic concept is the same: treating the hide with chemicals to preserve it, then filling it with some sort of body to restore the size and shape the creature had when it was alive.

In England in the early nineteenth century, animals were stuffed, literally; hence the expression "to stuff an animal." The skin of a creature was tightly crammed with dry leaves and moss. The skeleton was left inside to give something of the original shape. Later taxidermy progressed to the methods now universally used, although each taxidermist has his own personalized technique, developed and improved through trial and error.

In the beginning taxidermists had many obstacles to overcome. One problem was the tanning of hides. Tanning dates from the periods when clothing was improvised from skins. But for clothing the hair usually was removed, simply because ancient methods had no "tricks" for keeping the hair intact. In taxidermy everything about an animal's skin must remain the way it is. Various processes were sought to retain the hide's strength and hair and still give it pliability for stretching

on a form. Today this is no longer a problem. There are literally hundreds of methods of tanning hides for taxidermy work, many of them simple formulas. One of the most basic is known as "pickling." This process retains the hair and preserves the hide to keep it from cracking, decaying and deteriorating with age, yet the leather remains firm and will hold its shape once it is stretched tightly over the form. Instant dry and liquid preservatives alike are also available by mail order.

There is no hidden magic to successful taxidermy, no shortcut to success. As I discovered for myself, anyone, young or old, with average ability for working with his hands can transform a dead animal, bird or fish into a realistic mount.

Virtually everything required for home taxidermy can be obtained in a town that has a hardware store, lumber yard and grocery store. The list of essentials includes: pocketknife, screwdriver, drill, hammer, nails, string, excelsior (wood shavings), salt, borax, clay and alum. Take a bird, fish or animal, and with these supplies, and plenty of time and patience, you can be a do-it-yourself

1-1. Basic tools required to get started in taxidermy: saw, brush, hammer, knife, drill and screwdriver.

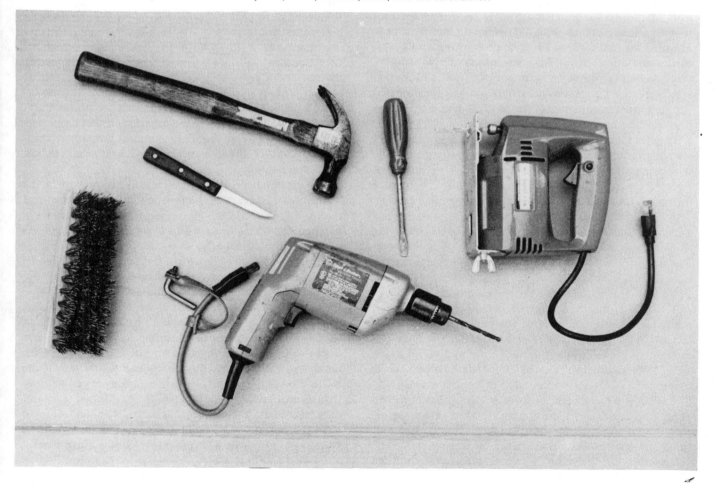

taxidermist. For more advanced taxidermy, you can order everything needed from the supply houses listed in the Appendix.

In some parts of the country home taxidermy is an ideal hobby for the shut-in season of winter. During other seasons you may collect specimens and freeze them until you are ready to mount them. A bird can be wrapped to give it some protection, and stored in the freezer. Wrap a fish in a damp cloth before freezing to prevent damage to the vulnerable tail and fins. A small animal, such as a squirrel, can be wrapped in heavy paper and frozen. Just freeze your specimens with innards intact and they will keep indefinitely.

There are five basic steps in creating a mount: 1. skinning; 2. curing of hide; 3. preparing the form, or mannequin, as taxidermists call it; 4. fitting the skin on the mannequin; 5. finishing. With fish, birds and small animals, the first four steps can be accomplished almost progressively, within a day's time. The exception is finishing. Each mount requires a drying-out period before it can be completed.

Each step is just as important as any other. A beginner can make taxidermy as simple or as difficult as he chooses. To simplify it, he may bypass the preparation of the mannequin. A form of correct shape and specifications can be purchased from a taxidermy supply house. This saves much time, since forming and sculpturing the mannequin involves hours of painstaking work. Whether you buy a mannequin or make your own, however, one item absolutely necessary to the finished product must be bought: this is the glass eyes. Everything else can be improvised at home.

The taxidermist must accomplish each progressive step in creating a mount with utmost care. By doing this, with a positive approach, he avoids making mistakes. Every little thing he does means something. A painter might splash an insignificant bit of paint on his canvas. This slight touch may seem unimportant at the time, but once the painting is completed, that spot of paint may be the highlight which gives the painting its "life." In taxidermy a minor error may be made while preparing the mannequin, a mistake which at the moment seems irrelevent. But by the time the mistake reaches the outside, in the finished mount, it can become magnified many times. The tendency of the beginner is to be too liberal. With my first big-game mount, I used far too much clay modeling the animal's nose and facial structures. When the mount was finished the deer had a chipmunk-like face, too rounded to appear exactly lifelike. This is why the emphasis is on detail, patience and care. The taxidermist must be observant, imaginative. But if you goof, don't be dismayed. Remember that quality work comes with patience and experience. The satisfaction lies in seeing improvement as you continue

to create different mounts at home.

The creative process begins with the first incision in the animal, fish or bird to be skinned. Removing the hide is the obvious first step. A taxidermist with average skill can take a creature that has been skinned properly and turn out a respectable mount, but not even the best of taxidermists can overcome the obstacles of a shoddy skinning job. The skin must be cut in the proper places, where the incisions are later hidden, and the cuts must be firm and clean so that the parts can be fitted back together neatly. The skin must be removed without excessive cuts and gashes. Once the skin is off, it must be cleaned and preserved. The mannequin must be made to exact specifications. The skin must be stretched and molded to the mannequin. And in finishing the taxidermist adds the final touches which give the mount a truly lifelike look.

The most important attributes of the taxidermist are skill with his hands and imagination. The taxidermist works entirely with his hands, fitting and stretching and molding the hide over the mannequin. Anyone who can build a miniature scale model from a kit has the dexterity needed to create a mount from a dead animal, fish or bird.

But taxidermy, strangely, must be impersonal. A wild bird actually has no specific intimate meaning to the taxidermist. Yet a household pet, either your own or someone else's, should never be mounted. To the owner the pet had a personality. This never can be recaptured in a mount. It is difficult enough to work with impersonal specimens, such as wild animals, without compounding your woes by using an animal that has a personal meaning to someone. In a mount you are attempting to capture the creature's physical characteristics, not its personality.

The imagination of the taxidermist shows up in the overall coordination of the finished mount. On the head mount of a deer, as one example, there must be a balance between the ears and eyes and nose. The eyes must be turned properly, so the mount appears natural and not cross-eyed. They must be focused in relation to the nose; if the eyes are turned one way and the nose another the animal appears unbalanced. The ears give the impression of the creature's being dead or alive, alert or relaxed. With a bird an overall balance is sought, in which the bird perches naturally on a branch and doesn't appear unsteady and about to topple off. Fish must flow in lines; one line compliments another. If the bottom or underside of the fish is gently curved and the top is crooked, the fish seems humpbacked and unnatural. What is involved, basically, is imagination to pose the mount in a lifelike manner. This may require studying photographs in magazines and nature books.

Of all creatures, a bird is the easiest to mount, a fish

1-2. A rainbow trout.

the most difficult. A bird is fairly simple to skin and any minor mistakes can be obscured with feathers. A bird also is the easiest of all wild creatures to obtain. Pheasant and quail are among the easiest birds to skin. If there is a bird farm in your community you can buy one of these birds, or maybe you can kill one on a hunting trip. Also fairly elementary is the pigeon. The beginner would be wise to start with a bird. Except for finishing, all the steps can be accomplished in one sitting. Even with birds you should not expect dramatic results with your first efforts. Quality comes with experience.

Rathbone recalls that a school teacher got him interested in taxidermy as a hobby. He was 11 years old at the time, a kid bursting with curiosity and ready to try anything challenging. He decided to mount a robin. He struggled through the first skinning job with some success. The hide was removed with only a few minor cuts. He was flushed with confidence. But he ruined his next half-dozen birds.

"I thought I knew it all," Rathbone explains. "I was in too big a hurry. I chopped the birds up. It took some frustrating blunders for me to realize the importance of painstaking care."

Just because a creature is small doesn't mean that it is necessarily easier to skin and mount. There comes a point when a mount is so small that the chore becomes more complex and difficult. Rathbone says that one of the most difficult mounts he ever created was from a week-old cottontail rabbit, a job he was to do for a museum. The animal was tiny and dainty. The skin was like wet tissue paper. He says he could have mounted an

entire deer in the time it required to bring that baby rabbit back to its original shape. And the deer job certainly would have been less frustrating.

Oversized specimens also compound the taxidermist's problem. A wild turkey is more difficult to mount than a

1-3. Just about any type of mannequin needed is available from a taxidermy supply house.

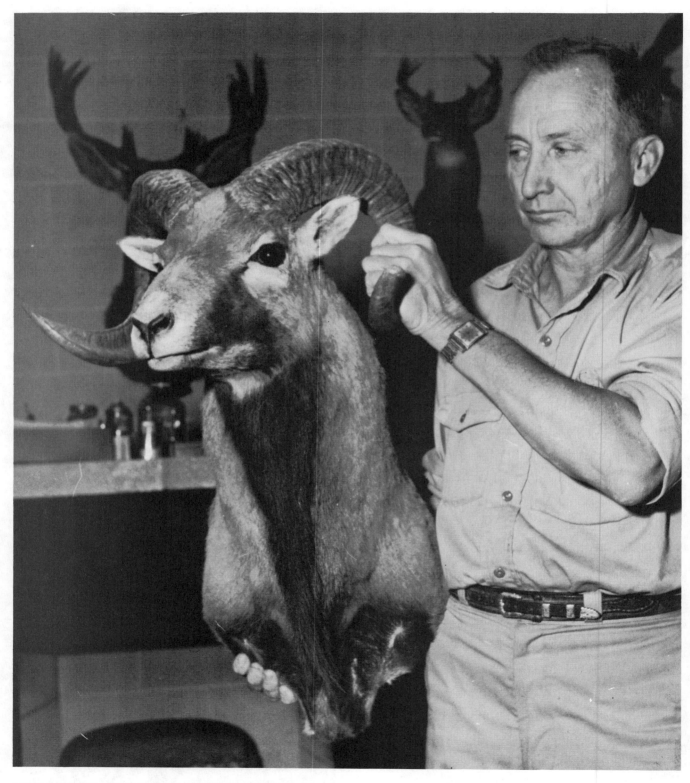

1-4. Lem Rathbone with head mount of a male mouflon (wild sheep).

1-8. Leser scaup duck (left) and spoonbill duck (right).

pheasant, and a sailfish is more difficult and much more expensive than a black bass. Medium-sized creatures are the easiest, and they also result in the best finished mounts. This is true of birds, animals or fish.

All this may seem involved and complicated; that is only because I want to prepare you for what is ahead. Taxidermy is fun, fascinating, but it isn't a casual, haphazard thing which can be rushed into without forethought and preparation. Creating a mount takes time, lots of time. Beyond the actual work involved, there will be time lapses with some specimens, such as several days for the hide of a big-game mount to cure in salt and later pickle in its special solution, and many

more days for it to dry out properly on the mannequin. You won't see results immediately. But taxidermy gives a certain inner satisfaction of accomplishment that few other hobbies can bring. Unlike the artist, the taxidermist is not duplicating a scene in another medium. He is taking the actual thing, a creation of nature, and attempting to re-create it to the very best of his ability. It could be compared to picking up a piece of the earth, shaking it violently, and asking someone to put all the pieces back in their original shape and perspective. It is literally impossible to get perfection, to re-create it actually as it was. But the fun and challenge is in trying.

2/Collecting Specimens

2/Collecting Specimens

You may remember that several robins were sacrificed to start Lem Rathbone on his future career as a professional taxidermist. "I would start skinning one," he recalls, "make a mistake, then go get me another bird and begin again. That's the way I learned, mostly by trial and error."

If you are inclined to criticize that confession, remember that when Rathbone was learning his trade there seemed to be an endless supply of robins—so many in fact that some people considered them pests. Taking a few for taxidermy purposes was no big deal.

Now times have changed, and virtually all living creatures are protected in one way or another. There are a few exceptions, such as the coyote, the starling and the English sparrow, but very few. It is the responsibility of the collector or the hunter to know which animals are protected and to obey all laws, especially those governing endangered species. Game birds can be legally taken only during designated open seasons; raptors and songbirds are protected by both federal and state laws.

The broad protective legal umbrella means that a raptor or songbird can be taken and mounted only by a person who has a scientific collector's permit. And only qualified professional taxidermists working in conjunction with a natural science center or museum, which must prove a public need, can get such a permit.

For a complete digest of federal bird-protective laws, write for the pamphlet entitled *Birds Protected by Federal Law*, issued by Fish and Wildlife Service, Bureau of Sport Fisheries and Wildlife, U.S. Department of Interior, Washington, D.C. 20240.

Federal law also requires a permit for performing taxidermy services on migratory birds for any person other than oneself. This means that if you mount a duck or dove or any other migratory bird for another person, you must have a permit, whether you charge for the service or not. Many states also require taxidermy permits, but primarily for professionals or those who charge for their services. The home-hobby taxidermist doesn't need a permit. Check with your state game and fish department to find out what you can and cannot do and whether you need a permit.

If your state requires a permit, this must be obtained before you apply for a federal permit, since the state permit number must be on the federal application. States charge for permits, and fees vary, as do requirements. The federal permit, for a two-year duration, is free. Write the Fish and Wildlife Service, at the address already given, to request an application for a Federal Fish and Wildlife Permit.

The penalities for violating the protective laws can be quite severe. Therefore, do not perform a taxidermy ser-

2-1. Mallard duck (drake).

vice for anyone else without obtaining the proper permits, and never mount a protected raptor or songbird for yourself or anyone else. The risks are too great. Buy pen-raised pheasants or quail, or obtain pigeons, or collect game birds during the legal open season.

If you hunt, you can stockpile game birds during open seasons and put them into the freezer until you are ready to mount them. If you decide on quail, for example, collect enough to allow you to make mistakes on a few and not worry about them.

As mentioned earlier, the way a specimen is collected and treated in the field will have a significant impact on the ultimate finished mount. You stand a much better chance of getting a lifelike mount with a bird in mint condition than with one that has been handled carelessly. Learning is difficult enough without compounding your woes with shoddy specimens.

Game birds, such as quail, should be taken with the smallest shot you can obtain (No. 9 in commercial shotshells). Carry some newspaper and package each bird individually, smoothing the feathers and rolling the bird loosely in a sheet of paper and securing it with a rubber band. Do this with each bird as soon as it is killed. Don't pitch all the birds together into a game bag and later attempt to repair the damage and package them. It is also helpful to have an ice chest in your car. You can then place the rolled birds in the chest and keep them cool until you can get them to a freezer.

Taxidermist Earl Griffith recommends an alternative for newspaper wrap in the form of old panty hose. First, though, be sure to wash any blood gently off the bird's feathers, preferably before it has dried. Once blood dries, it is difficult to remove. If the bird is bleeding from the mouth, place a wad of paper towel in the mouth. The paper will absorb the blood and keep it from drying around the mouth. Next, slip the bird head first into the panty hose, so that the feathers are snugged down properly. When removing the bird, remember to cut the hose open with scissors first; otherwise, the bird could be damaged.

With pheasants, Griffith cites the importance of keeping the tail straight. Once bent, it tends to take a set; as

2-2. **Sailfish.**

2-3. Scaled (blue) quail.

2-4. Western diamondback rattlesnake.

2-5. Javelina (collared peccary).

a result, the mount may not look as realistic as it should, despite your best taxidermy efforts. As Griffith points out, "Proper care and preservation are really only common sense."

The same kind of treatment should be given to small game animals—cottontail rabbits, squirrels—and even to fish. If you put a live fish in an ice chest, it will flounce wildly and damage its scales and skin. First wrap it in a wet towel (paper will stick to the slime and come to pieces, causing more problems than it solves). If you drag a fish—a bass, for example—around on a stringer, you will knock some scales loose and end up with an inferior mount.

When putting a fish into the freezer, keep it wrapped in a moist towel. The fish should not be gutted; freeze it as is, innards and all. Freezing the towel serves a twofold purpose: it keeps the fish moist and also serves as a cast, or support, protecting the fish as it is moved around in the freezer. Left unprotected, the frozen tail and fins could easily break.

Never put a bird, animal or fish in a sealed plastic bag unless you intend to refrigerate or freeze it immediately. And when putting the specimen on ice, be sure to leave the bag unsealed until all heat has escaped.

Never put any bird, animal or fish in a sealed plastic bag to refrigerate or freeze it.

"The plastic bag has been one of the biggest curses of modern taxidermy," Rathbone says. "Plastic eliminates all air circulation and promotes rapid spoilage. If you try to keep anything without ice in a plastic bag you are asking for trouble."

Rathbone recommends that, whenever possible, any animal or bird be collected with the smallest shotgun shot that will kill it quickly and humanely. Fur and hair will hide the tiny shot holes. They create no problems of repair.

2-6. Cottontail rabbit.

2-7. Canada goose.

2-8. Wild turkey.

However, suppose you are hunting deer and sight a big buck. At that moment you aren't thinking of taxidermy. You shoot the animal with a high-powered rifle bullet or shotgun slug that will leave a gaping hole. For this reason, condition yourself always to aim behind the animal's shoulder, in the lung and heart area. This will not damage the cape needed for the head mount. Do not shoot the animal in the head or neck.

Once your quarry is down, do not cut the throat or make any other unnecessary cuts. If time is limited, don't attempt a hurry-up skinning job. Wait until you can do it at leisure.

If the cape is badly damaged, try to find a substitute. If it is a deer, attempt to get a cape from another deer of similar size. The antlers are the trophy; the cape is only of secondary importance. Once the finished mount is hanging on the wall, no one except you will be the wiser. It isn't the source of the hide or cape that is important; rather, it is the completed mount. Use any trick or gimmick, natural or artificial, which will improve the finished product.

2-9. Fox squirrel.

2-10. Bobcat.

2-11. Raccoon.

2-12. Mourning dove.

2-13. White-winged dove.

2-14. Whitetail deer.

2-15. Jack rabbit.

2-16. A fish that you intend to mount should be put on ice immediately, but the specimen will be better protected if it is first wrapped in a wet towel or cloth.

2-17. Raptors such as this kestral are protected by both federal and state laws; never mount one for yourself or anyone else.

3/Basic Mounts

3/Basic Mounts

Now you can get started on taxidermy.

It is important that you blend much serious work with enthusiasm and imagination. We will begin by describing three fairly simple mounts, to allow you to get the "feel" of things. Just remember that successful taxidermy is a systematic, step-by-step process. There are no quick and simple shortcuts and you can not leap ahead and put a later step before an earlier one. Follow the outlined plan precisely, accomplishing each step to the best of your ability. Don't worry about successive steps; take one at a time. You are on your own. Any accomplishments you might have, depicted in a mount, will be the result of your own efforts. Often it is lonely, frustrating work, seemingly endless at times, but don't become discouraged. It is a proud day indeed when you can step back and look at your first mount. However it may turn out, it will be a part of you, and that alone justifies pride.

Antlers (or Horns) on a Plaque

Perhaps the best-known mount is a set of antlers or horns on a plaque. Despite its simplicity, you cannot approach this job haphazardly. It requires a certain amount of tedious work.

ANTLERS OR HORNS ON PLAQUE

TOOLS

Sharp knife	Glover's needle
Saw (meat or coping)	Hammer
Teaspoon	Screwdriver
2-gallon container	Drill with ¼-inch bit

SUPPLIES

4 pounds table salt
6-inch by 6-inch piece of ⅜-inch plywood
¼ pound alum
¼ pound 20 Mule Team Borax
[Note: in lieu of salt, alum or 20 Mule Team Borax, a quick preservative, either dry or liquid, can be used.]
4 No. 2 shingle nails
No. 8 linen thread
About 12 carpet tacks
2 1½-inch wood screws
Potter's clay or fire clay
1 pound plaster of Paris
   (for horned animals only)
Plaque
Screw eye

3-1. **Make a cut from the antler down, and from the side of the nose through the eye to the back of the head, on both sides.**

Step 1 —*Skinning*

Begin by skinning the head of the animal—deer, wild sheep, antelope, elk—to remove the scalp. Any sharp knife will do. A medium-sized pocketknife or skinning knife is the ideal size.

Insert the knife blade at the base of one antler or horn and cut downward through the skin, forward of the ear and behind the jaw. Go straight down the side of the face. After making this initial incision on one side, go to the other antler or horn and cut likewise down the opposite side of the face. Now you have two cuts, from the bases of both antlers or horns down the jaws.

Next, insert the blade point in the nose, parallel with the eye, and cut straight back, through the eye socket,

3-2. **Remove the skull plate by sawing from behind the antlers through the eye to middle of nose.**

on both sides, bisecting the downward cuts and going around the head until both incisions meet at the back *(illustration 3-1)*. If you are working with an antlered animal like a deer or an elk, take a screwdriver and loosen the skin carefully around the base of each antler. With horned animals like antelope, goats and wild sheep, the skin at the base of the horns must be severed with a knife. Peel the scalp off. Clean away any flesh, salt liberally with table salt or stock salt and rub the salt vigorously into the side of the hide without hair. It is imperative that the entire flesh side be covered with salt. Roll the scalp into a tight ball, the salted side in, and place in a cool, shaded area to cure. The hide should be left this way about 3 days.

Step 2 —*Removing Antlers or Horns*

An ordinary meat saw is best for removing the antlers or horns from the head, but any saw will suffice. Be absolutely sure it is sharp enough to give an even, smooth cut.

Begin at the back of the head, just behind the ears, and saw straight through, on a level plane, emerging at the front just above the nose *(illustration 3-2)*. The skull plate should be flat in order for it to rest evenly against the plaque once it is mounted. Take this piece of skull,

3-3. **Horned animals must have the horns removed from their cores and the cores cleaned.**

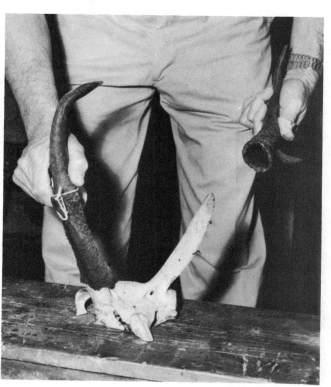

with antlers or horns attached, and clean away all flesh, including the brains.

Step 3 —*Pickling*

After cleaning the scalp, cure it with a dry or liquid quick preservative (following the instructions that come with it). Considering the time it takes to order and receive this material, however, pickling may in this instance prove faster.

Prepare the pickling solution by bringing a gallon of water to boil and adding 2 ¼ pounds of salt, one-quarter pound of alum and one-quarter pound of 20 Mule Team Borax. A grocery store should be able to provide these ingredients, but you may have to obtain the alum from a drugstore. Once the contents are completely dissolved, remove the solution from the stove and allow it to cool. After the salted hide has cured for the prescribed 3 days, unroll it and submerge it in the cooled pickling solution. Leave the hide in the solution for about a week, agitating it every other day. After a week, remove the hide and scrape away any membranes that remain inside the hide. An ordinary teaspoon is the best instrument for this job, using the rounded end. Now return the hide to the pickling solution until you are ready to use it.

Step 4 —*Preparation for Mounting*

Again, a quick preservative may be used. Simply freeze the scalp until you are ready for it. The method of preparation remains the same whether you use a quick preservative or opt for pickling.

3-4. The skull plate is attached to plywood with four nails, two in front of and two behind the antlers.

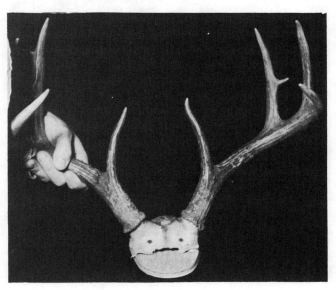

3-5. Clay or plaster of Paris is used to model the skull plate back to its natural contour.

While the hide is pickling, you can prepare the antlers or horns for mounting. Antlers can be mounted as they are, but horns require some special preparation. Take the skull plate with the horns attached, put it in a pail of water and boil for about an hour, or until the horns become loose. Pull them off their cores. Inside will be a skin-like growth, which is really new horns growing. Peel this away entirely, leaving only the solid bases *(illustration 3-3)*.

The difference between antlers and horns, incidentally, is that antlers are solid bone and are shed and regrown annually, while horns are more permanent and are never shed, the one exception being the pronghorn (antelope). The pronghorn, like antlered animals, sheds and regrows his horns each year and no other horned animal in the world does this. Antlered animals include deer, elk, moose and caribou. Regardless of the size of the antlers, they are dropped and a new set promptly commences growing. The antler is the fastest-growing bone known. Horns are found on such animals as pronghorn, cattle, sheep and goats.

Mix plaster of Paris, fill the horns and push them securely back on the cores. The mixture should be thin; otherwise the horns won't go back on completely. Unless this is accomplished, the inside of the horns will eventually rot and the mount will be ruined.

Next take the piece of three-eighths-inch plywood, trace the skull plate on the board and; with a coping

3-6. The scalp, left, goes back on the contoured skull plate, right.

saw, cut it out. Remove the front half of the skull plate and attach the remainder (the part with the antlers) to the plywood, using four No. 2 shingle nails (one just in front of and one just behind each antler), nailing through the skull into the board *(illustration 3-4)*. Bend the nails over in back to secure the antlers tightly to the plywood. Now mold the contour of the head back to its original shape with clay—plaster of Paris can be substituted, but it is more difficult to work with—being careful that you do not use too much clay or plaster *(illustration 3-5)*. Potter's clay or fire clay is best and can be obtained at a lumber yard. Do not use clay with an oil base, such as is sold at hobby shops. The oil will eventually soak through the hide. The idea is to replace the flesh with clay to give a lifelike shape and contour to the head. A small paint brush dipped in water can be used to smooth the clay. With plaster of Paris, an old table knife is a good sculpturing tool.

Step 5 —*Mounting*

Remove the scalp from the pickling solution and wash it in cool water with powdered detergent to remove the pickle. Afterward, rinse the scalp in cool water to get rid of the soap. Now with the scalp and sculptured antlers

3-7. The hide is to be sewed down about 2 inches at the base of each antler.

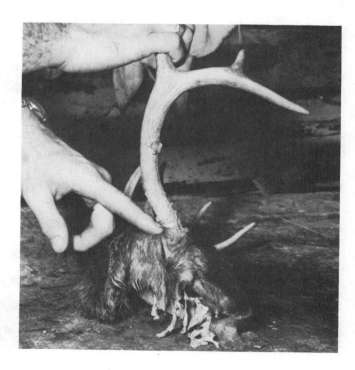

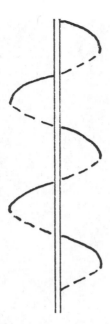

3-8. The needle goes into the incision and out the hide each time, rather than down through the hair.

you are ready for the actual mounting *(illustration 3-6)*.

After the scalp has drained but while it is still wet, put it back in place on the contoured skull plate. If it doesn't fit smoothly without wrinkles, add more clay to build up the contour; should it be too snug, scrape some of the clay away. Get the scalp to fit as naturally as possible.

Once you have the scalp smoothly and snugly on the skull plate, sew up the incisions, from the antlers or horns down *(illustration 3-7)*. This involves about a 2-inch sewing job on each side. The best needle for this is a glover's needle, available at a saddle shop, but an ordinary heavy-duty sewing needle can be used, although it is somewhat more difficult to work with. The glover's is a special three-cornered needle with sharp edges, which can be drawn through leather. Don't pull this needle through your fingers; it cuts. The best thread is linen, No. 8 or larger. Linen is durable and won't rot.

Stitch by passing the needle through the cut, then bringing the thread over into the incision, out the other side, and back in the incision again. This way you always push the needle through from the flesh side, rather than down through the hair. The thread never

3-9. The hide is tacked on the back of the plywood and the surplus is trimmed away.

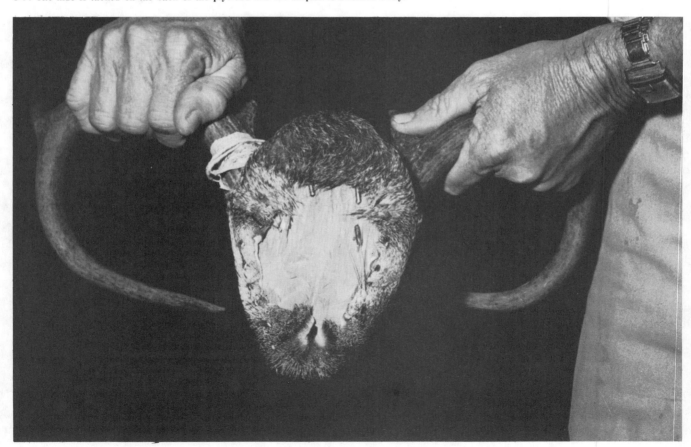

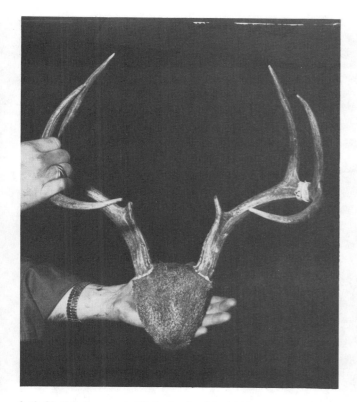

3-10. Skull plate covered with the deer's original scalp.

3-11. Skull plate covered with tanned leather.

goes across the incision, bridging it, but always along each side and through the incision. This stitch causes the leather to lie flat instead of buckling, making the sewing least noticeable *(illustration 3-8)*.

After sewing, the loose ends of the scalp will fall naturally around the plywood base. Fold the surplus hide underneath and tack it to the back side of the plywood, using common carpet tacks spaced about one-half inch apart. When the tacking is finished, the surplus skin can be trimmed away *(illustration 3-9)*. Now the covered skull should be put aside to dry for about 10 days.

This mount involves the original skull scalp *(illustration 3-10)*. But either tanned leather or felt can be substituted *(illustration 3-11)*. Tanned leather can be obtained from a hobby shop, local taxidermist or saddle shop.

A rectangular 6- by 8-inch piece of leather will suffice for deer, antelope and other animals of this size, while one of about 12 by 14 inches is needed for elk and one of 12 by 18 inches for moose. Lay the leather flat and determine where the antlers or horns will go, positioning them so that they are centered over the skull plate. Mark the spot for one antler and, using a sharp knife, cut a straight line from this mark out to the edge of the leather. Carve a small hole where the base of the antler

or horn will go, making it smaller than the antler or horn base. This way you'll get a tighter fit. Put the leather in place, pulling the cut hole around the antler or horn base snugly and stretching the leather so that it is smooth over the skull plate. Mark the position of the

3-12. Antlers go on a plaque that is hung with an eye screw.

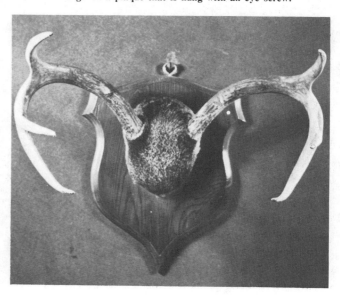

other antler or horn and cut another small hole and a straight line out to the edge of the leather. This incision should be directly opposite the first one.

Now thoroughly wet the leather and prepare to position it on the skull plate. Wet leather is easily stretched and upon drying will shrink slightly to give a smoother fit over the plate. Fit the leather tightly around the antler or horn bases (shrinkage will tend to pull it away from the base unless it is tight) and sew on each side, down from the bases about 2 inches. Now tuck the surplus leather underneath and tack it on the plywood base with carpet tacks, afterward trimming the excess.

The same procedure can be followed with felt, although you do not wet the felt.

Felt can be bought from a dry-goods store or ordered from a mail-order catalog; it comes in a wide variety of colors. Felt is easier to work with than leather because it has more stretch.

Step 6 —*Finishing*

You can order a suitable mounting plaque from any of the supply sources listed in the appendix. Plaques come in a variety of sizes, shapes and colors, and prices

3-13. Pair of mouflon horns mounted on a plaque using buckskin.

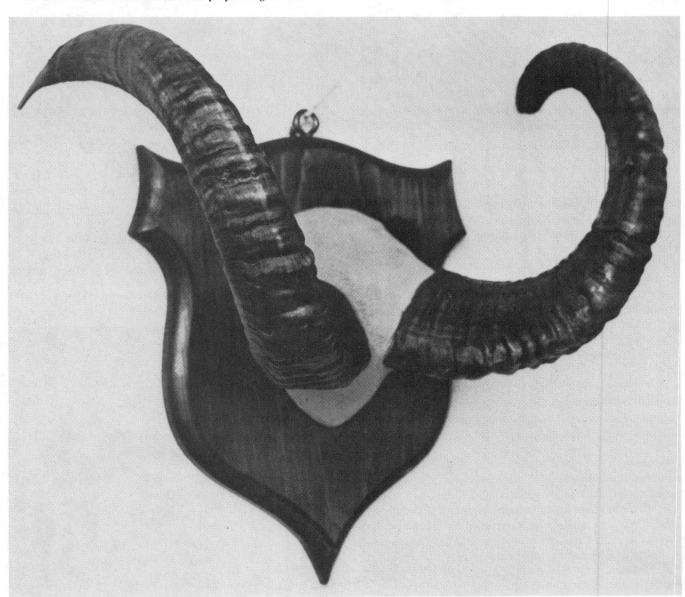

```
        PLASTIC FISH

TOOLS
1 ¼-inch paintbrush
3 small artist's paintbrushes
Small block wood
1-gallon container
Old kitchen knife


SUPPLIES
No. 1 molding plaster
Flat pan or box larger than the fish
Sand
Small can shellac
Petroleum jelly
Turpentine
Beeswax
4-inch piece of heavy wire
1 pint marine resin and catalyst (hardener)
Cheesecloth (optional)
1 cup shredded asbestos
Sandpaper
Various shades of paint needed
   to color fish
```

Plastic Fish

Any fish can be used for this mount, although with a scaled fish, such as a bass, a fish about 1 pound to 3 pounds in size is easiest to work with. Try one this size for a start and later you can graduate to bigger, more difficult mounts.

Step 1 —*Molding*

Get a flat pan or box longer than the fish and about 3 inches deep or deeper. Fill the container with sand. Lay the fish on the sand and bury half of it, leaving one side, the tail and the dorsal fin exposed.

With a block of wood pat around the fish, smoothing the sand *(illustration 3-14)*. Position the fins and tail flat on the sand, in the position you want them to appear on the finished cast. Fill the mouth with sand *(illustration 3-15)*. Stand back and look at the fish to determine that everything is in place naturally. Some of the fins may have to be pulled out and the tail may spread.

The fish should be completely ready to accept the plaster before the mixing is started. It pays to spread out newspapers and put the pan or box on them. Once you are finished you can simply throw away the papers. This saves a lot of fuss and bother afterward.

Obtain some No. 1 molding plaster. This is available in 100-pound sacks from lumber yards or in smaller quantities from a drugstore, but the bulk size is about as cheap at the lumber yard as is a 10-pound sack from a pharmacy. Get a 1-gallon can for mixing. Pour in 1 quart of cool water. Add plaster until the water completely disappears. Work the plaster with your hands until you get a consistency about like pancake batter. If the mixture is too thick, add more water; if it is thin, add plaster. But don't dally. This plaster dries extremely fast and haste is mandatory.

Once the plaster is mixed, immediately pour it over the half-buried fish *(illustration 3-16)*, until the fish is thoroughly covered *(illustration 3-17)*. After the plaster gets hard, or in about 10 minutes, mix more plaster and pour another application over the original coat. This makes the mold heavier and more durable. Allow it to set for at least 30 minutes (longer for slow-drying plaster). The longer you allow it to set, the better. The plaster should be totally dry.

Now gently pick up the plaster and turn it over *(illustration 3-18)*. The mold is delicate; handle it with extreme care. If the molding job is good, an exact impression of the fish will be in the plaster *(illustration 3-19)*. Wash the mold thoroughly and put it aside to dry while you prepare to make the cast.

Do not confuse the terms mold and cast. In a way they are like the negative and the print in photography.

are reasonable. Or you can improvise your own. Draw a design of your choice on a piece of cardboard and scissor it out as a pattern. Trace this on a board—pine, walnut or oak, depending on the quality of the plaque desired. Pine is cheapest and can be stained to almost any desired color. Cut it out with a band saw or coping saw. It can be left with a straight line (just sand the edges smooth) or the edge can be sculptured for a more decorative result. A router can give a rounded edge. Most lumber yards have routers and can do this job for you. Stain the plaque with a good grade of stain, in the color of your choice.

Determine where the antlers will go on the plaque, placing them and moving them around until they appear natural and balanced. Since most antlers are not perfectly symmetrical, they may have to be positioned slightly off-center to appear natural. Mark the spot where they go and in the center of this mark bore two holes about 2 inches apart. These holes should be no larger than one-quarter inch in diameter. Now anchor the antlers to the plaque by inserting flat-head wood screws from the back, through the bored holes into the plywood base of the antlers or horns. A small eye-bolt can be screwed atop the plaque for mounting *(illustration 3-12)*.

3-14. The fish is half-buried in sand and the sand is leveled with a block of wood.

3-15. The sand should be smooth around the fish and the fish's mouth should be filled.

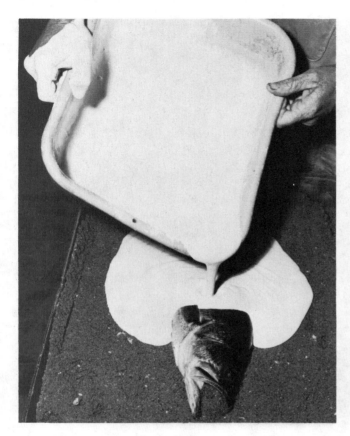 

3-16. Plaster is poured evenly over the entire fish.

3-17. The fish should be completely hidden by the plaster.

3-18. After the plaster dries the mold with the fish inside can be turned over.

3-19. This is the way the mold will look after the fish is removed.

3-20. A light coat of shellac is brushed in the inside of the mold.

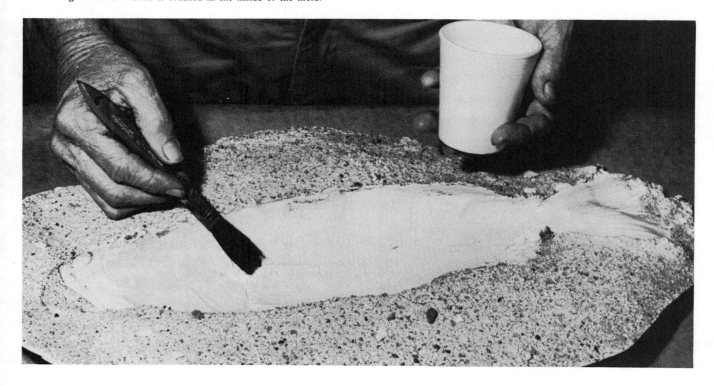

The mold is the negative, with everything in reverse, as you would see it in a mirror. When something is poured into this mold, you get a positive, the print, which is the exact replica of the original. This is the cast.

The mold is an important factor to the taxidermist when working with fish. Even when making a natural mount, as described in chapter 6, it pays to make a mold of the specimen first. You can later use it when sculpturing the mannequin, as a guide for both size and flow of lines. By making a cast of each side, you even can use papier-mâché (see appendix for formulas) to improvise a mannequin, putting the papier-mâché inside each side to get duplicates, then gluing them together to get the properly shaped body.

Step 2 —*Casting*

After the mold has completely dried, brush the inside of it lightly with shellac *(illustration 3-20)*, making sure you reach every crease. The coat must be extremely light so it won't obscure any of the detail.

When the shellac has dried, with your fingers rub a grease separator thoroughly over the inside of the mold. Ordinary petroleum jelly can be used, but you'll get a better job by mixing petroleum jelly, turpentine and beeswax in equal parts. This spreads more easily and allows more detail to reach the cast. Be sure you get it in every crease *(illustration 3-21)*. After you have finished, take a dry cloth and rub the inside of the mold, to remove any excess separator.

Now take the pint of resin (obtained from any hobby or boat shop) and add three drops of catalyst (hardener), which is available from the same sources. To this add 1 cup shredded asbestos, which you can get from a lumber yard or any place that sells household insulation. Stir the mixture until you get a smooth blend. The asbestos keeps the resin from running, making it easier to shape it inside the mold when making the cast.

Pour the resin into the mold and with a kitchen knife spread it evenly throughout *(illustration 3-22)*. The resin needs to be only about one-quarter inch thick all over, except for the fins and tail for which it is thinner. Resin is expensive and much waste occurs if the mold is filled entirely.

Be sure that the resin is spread everywhere you want an impression. To give the tail and fins some support, spread a thin coat of resin over them, add a chunk of cheesecloth to each part (with the tail, cut the cheesecloth to the same shape, only slightly smaller), and spread some more resin over this. The cheesecloth helps keep the fins and tail from breaking.

Bend the piece of wire into a U-shape and place it along the back, for a hanger. The bent part should extend slightly above the fish's back (you can hide it behind the dorsal fin). If the wire is bent inward, or toward you, the U-shape won't rest against the dorsal fin and stick to it. Put the hanger in balance with the whole fish so that the mount won't hang lopsided when you display it. Should you prefer a plaque, instead of using the hanger, put a block of wood about 3 inches long and 2 inches deep (or whatever size will fit) inside the fish and spread a little resin around its perimeter to hold it. Later, screws can be placed through the plaque into this block of wood to anchor the two together.

If the sun is shining, place the mold in the sun; the resin will "set up" quicker. After the resin is hard, carefully peel it from the mold, being careful not to break the cast. If the cast and mold do not separate easi-

3-21. A grease separator is rubbed over the dried shellac.

3-22. Resin with shredded asbestos added is smoothed in the mold.

ly, you may have to chip some of the mold away. The cast should be an exact replica of the fish you molded earlier *(illustration 3-23)*. Drying may require several hours.

Step 3 —*Finishing*

Trim the edges of the cast and sandpaper them. Some of the cast may have to be trimmed away to make sure it will lie flat against the wall. See chapter 7 for painting instructions.

Plaster Fish

Follow the instructions for the plastic fish for making a mold. Varnish and wax the inside of the mold, but instead of resin use plaster to make the cast. As plaster is much more likely to break than resin, fill the entire cavity with plaster. Cheesecloth support on the fins and tail is mandatory. Be extra careful when removing the plaster cast from the mold, as plaster chips easily. The process is identical except you are substituting plaster for resin. Trim, sandpaper and paint as you did with the plastic fish.

3-23. The plastic cast readily comes from the mold after it dries.

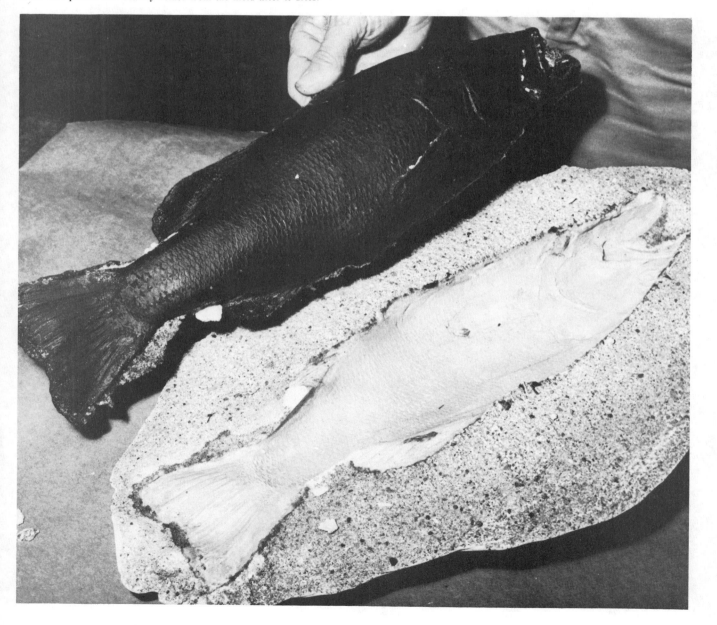

4/Birds

4/Birds

Now that you have had some practice with basic mounts, you are ready to mount or "stuff" a bird. The bird was selected for the first full mount because, of all wild creatures, it is the easiest to work with. Before you start working, however, read this chapter through completely and analyze it.

A bird of the right type is not difficult to skin; the form or mannequin is not complicated to make; and with the finished mount you have some flexibility in correcting errors that materialize as you put the final touches to your creation.

Choose a day when you have many successive hours in which to work. With a bird you can advance immediately through all the steps of actual mounting, with no time lapses. The skin actually cures on the mannequin. Time will be required to allow the mount to dry before you can finish it, but you'll see immediate results.

As a guide we will work with a pheasant, although there are several birds just as easy to mount. Except for differences in size, all the mounting of birds are basically the same, although some are easier to work with than others.

Falling within the "easy" category are quail, pheasant, hawk, pigeon, owl, road runner, crow and magpie. Classified as "difficult" are the various ducks, geese, chickens, turkeys and buzzards. With your first efforts you'll perhaps wonder how we could ever hang an "easy" label on the pheasant (or maybe the quail or pigeon). But with some experience you'll discover why. Birds of this group are fairly uncomplicated to skin and they are not so small as to make the work meticulous. A bird can be defined as "difficult" for several reasons. With ducks and geese, the skin is difficult to remove. You almost have to peel it away with a knife, cutting constantly. Chickens and turkeys have bare heads, which compounds the problem of creating a lifelike mount.

After you've mastered the techniques of mounting a bird in the easy category you may want to graduate to the difficult class. But begin with an easy one. You'll encounter enough problems without making your woes more acute with a bird that is difficult to work with.

Step 1 —*Skinning*

This is the most difficult step; once the bird is skinned, more than half the battle is won. It takes time and patience to peel away the skin with few mistakes. Allow yourself plenty of time.

The ingredients needed for this step are a small and sharp pocketknife, a box of 20 Mule Team Borax and some cotton. A small knife is much easier to use than a

BIRDS
(Pheasant)

TOOLS
Sharp knife
Paintbrush
Pliers
Drill with ¼-inch bit
Saw

SUPPLIES
Ball of twine
Quilting cotton
20 Mule Team Borax
Excelsior (wood shavings)
[Note: instead of building a body with twine and excelsior, you can substitute a ready-made urethane form (see Appendix for list of supply houses).]
Ordinary sewing needle
No. 8 thread
No. 10 galvanized wire
  2 pieces 14 inches long
  1 piece 20 inches long
  1 piece 12 inches long
No. 12 wire, 2 pieces, each 16 inches long
Glass eyes (to be ordered)
¼ pound fire clay
Oil paint
Varnish or clear fingernail polish
Perch (to be cut from branch)

large one. Just be sure it is sharp.

Spread out newspapers and lay the bird on its back on the papers. Stuff some cotton in its mouth to prevent any bleeding on the feathers. If there are any bad wounds, close these with cotton. Sprinkle borax on any fresh blood which might be on the feathers. The idea is to keep the bird as dry as possible at all times. This prevents the soiling of feathers and will result in a quality mount.

Spread the feathers and make a short incision from the breastbone down to the vent. Do not cut any feathers. Now gingerly spread the skin back in both directions, opening the incision (illustration 4-1). Grasp one side and slowly peel the skin toward the leg. As you expose the skin, keep sprinkling it with borax to remove the moisture. The borax also acts as an agent to cure the skin. Be liberal with the powder. Any excess on the feathers can be brushed away later.

Slowly separate the skin and flesh with your fingers until you reach the legs. The belly part of the bird will now be exposed. Grasping the left leg with your right

hand, stick the first two fingers of your left hand under the skin and carefully peel it over the leg joint. Sever the leg at the joint (illustration 4-2). Now, on the opposite side, hold the leg with your right hand and with your left pull the skin away, exposing the joint. Cut this leg free. Keep peeling the skin away until you reach the base of the tail. Here the tail is to be severed; (illustration 4-3) but be very careful not to cut close to the large tail feathers. If you should cut the ends, the feathers will easily slip out. Cut just forward of the tail feather roots, separating the tail from the body. The entire lower part of the body is now exposed.

The next step is to skin forward on the body, peeling back the skin until you reach the bases of the wings. Keep sprinkling the exposed side of the skin liberally with borax. Skin up both wings to where the large feathers start. Now sever the wings at the shoulders, where they are attached to the bird's body (illustration 4-4). Keep working forward until you come to the neck. Skin to the base of the skull and cut the neck (illustration 4-5).

On some birds you'll be able simply to reverse the skin of the neck, wrong side out, and peel it over the head (illustration 4-6). But if the fit is too tight, making skinning difficult, you may have to cut a slit in the throat (illustration 4-7) to get at the head.

As you skin the head, the first real trouble spot will be an ear socket. The ears can be pulled from the skull with your fingernails. When you come to the eyes, be extra cautious when cutting around the sockets. Avoid nicking the eyelids. Once the eye sockets are loose, pull the skin down to the bill. Do not cut around the bill. The entire skull should remain clinging to the skin (illustration 4-8).

Clean the skull by removing all the flesh, including the eyes and tongue and the flesh around the jaw bones. Be liberal with the borax. Enlarge the hole in the back of the head, remove the brains and sprinkle the inside of the cavity with borax. The skull should be completely clean but still affixed to the hide.

Now return to the wings. Lay the wings out flat, undersides exposed. Each wing is composed of three distinct joints. By flexing the wing you can determine where these are. Peel back the skin until you come to the first joint (illustration 4-9). Just forward of this joint make a short incision in the wing, from this joint to the next one. Peel back the skin slightly on either side and clean away all the flesh around the bone, being careful not to cut through the wing. When this is completed, make another short incision forward of this joint to the tip of the wing and clean away all the flesh around the bone. Sprinkle borax liberally in both incisions. Remove all flesh from the big bone at the base of the wing (illustration 4-10).

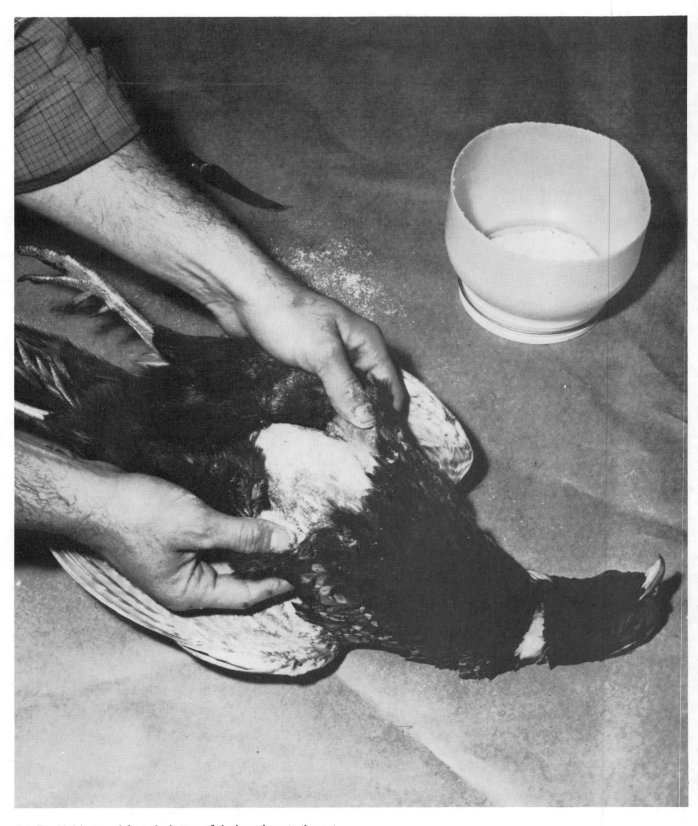

4-1. The bird is opened from the bottom of the breastbone to the vent.

Follow the same procedure on the other wing, skinning from where the wing was cut from the body up to the first joint, then making two incisions, one between this joint and the next, and the second from the last joint to the tip of the wing.

With the legs, skin down as far as the feathers go *(illustration 4-11)*. Completely clean all the flesh from both leg bones *(illustration 4-12)*. With a pheasant this skinning job will go only to the knee joint, but with some birds, such as owls, the feathers grow much farther down the legs.

Skin down the tail base slightly and scrape away all the flesh *(illustration 4-13)*. Be careful not to sever the ends of the large tail feathers.

Be sure the bird is turned inside out, with the two large leg bones, the two large wing bones, the skull and the base of the tail exposed. All the exposed skin should be sprinkled liberally with borax. Turn the skin back to normal, with the feathers on the outside, put it aside and prepare for the next step.

Step 2 —*Making the Mannequin*

Necessary items for preparing a mannequin are excelsior and a small ball of twine. Excelsior, which is fine wood shavings used for packing fresh fruits and furniture, can be obtained at a grocery or furniture store. The twine should be light, the kind used for flying kites.

Begin by wadding some excelsior into a small ball, then wrapping this tightly with twine. Add a little more excelsior, then more twine, slowly building up your mannequin *(illustration 4-14)*. Use the original bird's body for a guide as to the size. The tendency is to build up the body too quickly. Just a thin layer of excelsior should be added each time. This makes the body firm and durable. When it is just slightly smaller than the original body (it should be egg-shaped), place it inside the skin and determine if it fits. The incision should come together with some slack left in the skin. Cotton will be used later to fill out the natural contour. If the skin fits too snugly the feathers won't lie naturally.

4-2. Each leg is severed from the body at the joint.

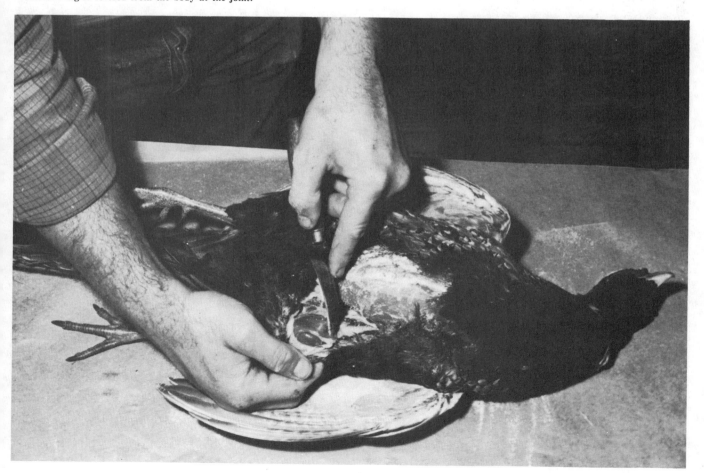

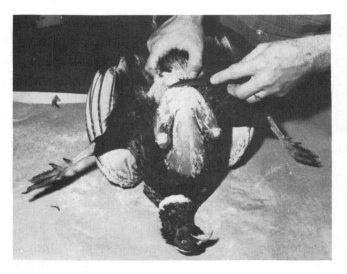

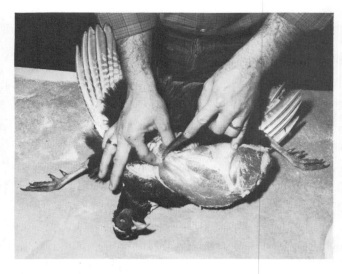

4-3. When severing the tail, be careful not to cut the roots of the long feathers.

4-4. Each wing is separated close to the body.

4-5. The neck is cut from the body at the base of the skull.

4-6. On some birds the neck can simply be turned back and the skull skinned.

4-7. But if the head won't come through the neck opening, you may have to make a short incision in the throat.

4-8. The skinned skull should be left attached to the skin at the bill.

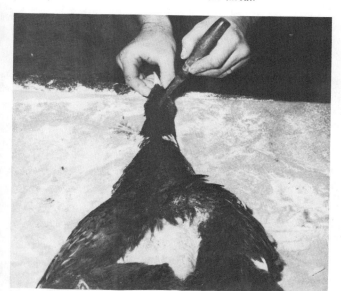

4-9. Skin each wing up to the joint where the large feathers begin.

4-10. Then completely clean the flesh off this large bone.

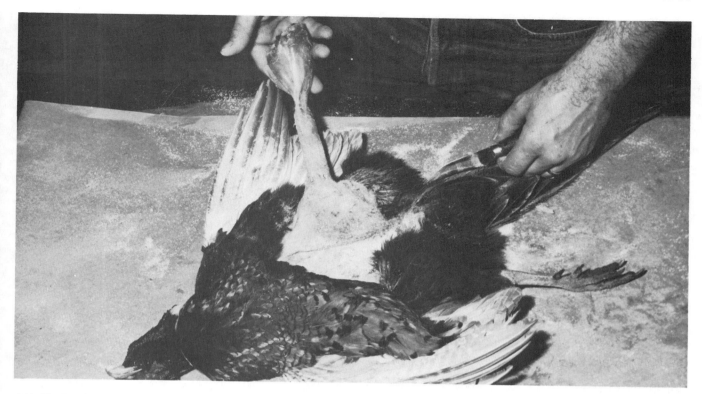

4-11. The leg should be skinned out to where the feathers end.

4-12. Remove all the flesh off this large leg bone.

4-13. Remove the chunk of flesh at the base of the tail, avoid cutting feathers.

4-14. A body is improvised by wrapping twine around excelsior.

If you decide not to make the body, or you can't find any excelsior locally, you can order a urethane form from a taxidermy supply house simply by specifying the species of bird. The mounting procedure with either type body is the same. As with excelsior, you will need to use cotton to fill out the natural contour. Taxidermist Jimmy Bird says that when he makes a urethane bird form (See Chapter 13, *Sculpturing*) he purposely makes it slightly undersized. He then packs cotton around the form to assure a snug, natural look. The final result is a finished mount with a more lifelike appearance.

Step 3 —*Mounting*

For mounting you'll need an ordinary sewing needle, No. 8 sewing thread, the necessary lengths of wire, (see table) a pair of glass eyes (see appendix) and a small amount of fire clay or modeling clay (without oil base). You must also have two pieces of No. 10 wire 14 inches long for the legs, and one piece 20 inches long for the neck. For a closed-wing mount, you'll need two 16-inch lengths of No. 12 wire; if the wings are to be spread, substitute heavier No. 10 wire. For the first mount we recommend that you make a closed-wing bird; it's easier. You'll also need about a 12-inch piece of No. 10 wire for a tail support.

WIRES NEEDED FOR VARIOUS BIRD MOUNTS

PHEASANT, SMALL HAWKS, DUCKS
No. 10 wire: 2 pieces, each 14 inches in length (legs); 1 piece 20 inches long (neck).
No. 10 wire: 2 pieces, each 16 inches in length (wing wires for open wing mount).
No. 12 wire: 2 pieces, each 16 inches (closed wing mount).
No. 12 wire: 1 piece 12 inches in length (tail support).

PIGEON
No. 12 wire: 2 pieces, 14 inches long (legs).
No. 14 wire: 2 pieces, 18 inches long (wings); 1 piece 12 inches long (neck).
No. 12 wire: 1 piece 10 inches long (tail support).

QUAIL, BLUEJAY
No. 14 wire: 2 pieces, 10 inches long (legs).
No. 20-22 wire: 2 pieces, 12 inches long (wings); 1 piece 10 inches long (neck).
No. 14 wire: 1 piece, 8 inches long (tail support).

LARGE HAWKS, OWLS, GEESE
No. 9 wire: 2 pieces, 20 inches long (legs); 1 piece 14 inches long (neck).
No. 12 wire: 2 pieces, 24 inches long (wings).
No. 9 wire: 1 piece, 14 inches long (tail support).

WILD TURKEY
¼-inch cold rolled steel rod: 2 pieces, 24 inches long (legs).
No. 9 wire: 2 pieces, 36 inches long (wings); 1 piece, 30 inches long (neck).
No. 9 wire: 1 piece 20 inches long (tail support).

You can obtain the glass eyes either from a local taxidermist or from any of the supply sources listed in the appendix.

Take one of the 16-inch pieces of No. 12 wire and sharpen one end. Starting at the first joint of the wing, the one nearest the end of the wing bone severed from the body, insert the sharp end of the wire between the skin and bone and slowly push it along the wing. The wire must follow the lay of the bone. Should you push the wire through the skin, draw it out and start again. The wire should be shoved the full length of the wing, all the way to the tip. A large piece of the wire will remain exposed, jutting out alongside the main wing bone, at the point where it was severed from the bird's body.

With the needle and No. 8 sewing thread close the two incisions in the underside of the wing. Nothing needs to be stuffed inside. Just sew shut snugly. Always sew from the inside out—that is, push the needle into the incision, then up through the skin, and over and down into the incision again, and so forth. If you attempt to sew down, through the feathers, the thread will bind and break.

Follow the same procedure with the other wing. When the four incisions, two in each wing, are closed, take the exposed ends of the wires and twist each one once around the large wing bone (illustration 4-15). Some exposed wire will still jut forward of the bone. This wire will be used to affix the wings to the body. In all, there should be roughly 12 inches of exposed wire beyond the bone.

Now take the excelsior body and push the 20-inch length of No. 12 wire into it about where you think the neck should be. Wrap some cotton around the wire, then wrap the cotton with twine, following the same routine used in making the body. Make the neck the same size as the one removed, working carefully to be sure that it is not oversized. Several inches of naked wire should extend forward of this improvised neck (illustration 4-16). Measure against the skin and try to get the cotton neck approximately the same length as the pheasant's neck.

Back to the skin again: using clay, fill the eye sockets smooth and round. Also use clay to pack the brain cavity, rounding the top of the head naturally. The eyes can be added now, or they can be put in later. The molded head (illustration 4-17) should fold back into the skin naturally.

Take the exposed wire jutting forward of the neck and insert it into the base of the skull, where this was attached to the original neck, and push the wire into the brain cavity. If the wire is too long, ram it through the head, out the top. Later you can clip off the excess.

Position the body in the skin and push the two wing wires diagonally into the body, one on each side (illustration 4-18). Use the original body as a guide to determine exactly where the wings go. The wires should protrude completely through the body and out the other side. Pull the wing bone on either side snugly against the body, bend the wires around the breast of the bird and twist them together. This holds both wings firmly in place. Bend the ends of the wire back in a horseshoe shape and push them back in the body, to hide the wires and eliminate the sharp ends.

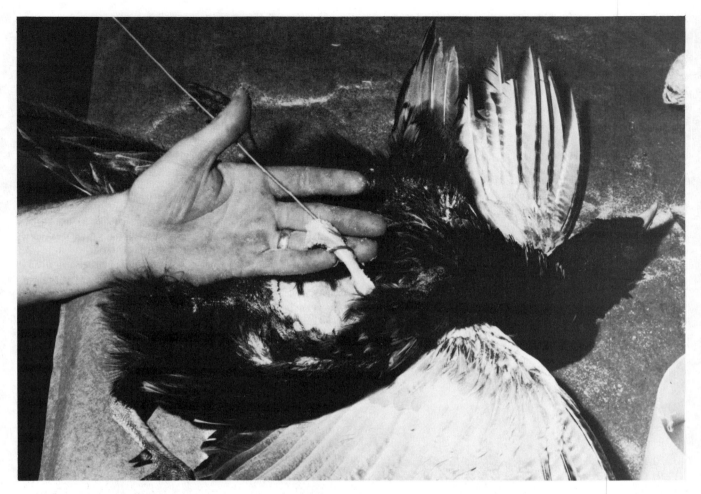

4-15. The wing wire should be attached by making one wrap around the bone.

4-16. The body has a cotton-covered neck with some bare wire extending from the end.

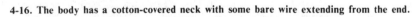

Now the head and wings are affixed. Next attach the legs. Take a 14-inch piece of No. 10 wire and sharpen one end. With the tip of your knife blade bore a tiny hole in the bottom of one foot. Insert the sharpened end of the wire and begin pushing it up the leg, along the shin bone, underneath the skin, on the back side of the leg. Pass the wire behind the heel bone up past the knee joint and alongside the exposed leg bone. Wrap the wire against the bone, using two or three turns of twine, *(illustration 4-19),* but do not wrap it tightly. The wire should slide up and down. Follow the same procedure on the other leg. With birds that have large thighs (drumsticks), some cotton must be wrapped around the large exposed bone to replace the flesh that was removed.

Using the original body as a guide, position the legs in place. On a pheasant the leg will go about in the middle of the body, in length and depth right from bottom up. Push the wires up and into the body, all the way through and out the other side. Make a hairpin turn in each end and push the exposed ends of wire back into the body. Grasp the end of the wire sticking out of the foot and with the other hand push the leg snugly against the body. Now the leg can be bent slightly to bind the wire and keep it from sliding back. This keeps the leg firmly against the body. Do this with both legs.

Fill around the excelsior body with quilting cotton. This cotton comes in sheets and is available at most dry-goods stores. Other cotton tends to lump as you attempt to stuff it around the body. Pull the main belly incision closed. If it is too tight, remove some cotton; if it is loose, add just a bit of cotton so that you can pull it together without effort, yet it will be snug *(illustration 4-20).* Now you are ready to close the cut. Sew from the vent, moving forward to the base of the breast bone, sewing in and out, as previously instructed.

Bend the 12-inch length of No. 10 wire into a horseshoe shape. Insert the ends just underneath the tail and push them into the body. Leave about a third of the wire, the curved end, sticking out. The tail rests on this, which provides support so the tail won't break off.

Improvise some sort of perch. One type is a limb that extends out from the wall *(illustration 4-21).* This is made by cutting a short section of limb with another smaller limb growing out from it. A screw eye goes into the end of the larger section, and the back side of the limb should be flattened so that it will rest firmly against a wall. Bore holes through the limb to affix the wires jutting from the bottom of the bird's feet, positioning it naturally.

Another perch can be a small stump cut from a portion of a limb *(illustration 4-22).* The size of the perch

4-17. Model the head with clay and position the glass eyes.

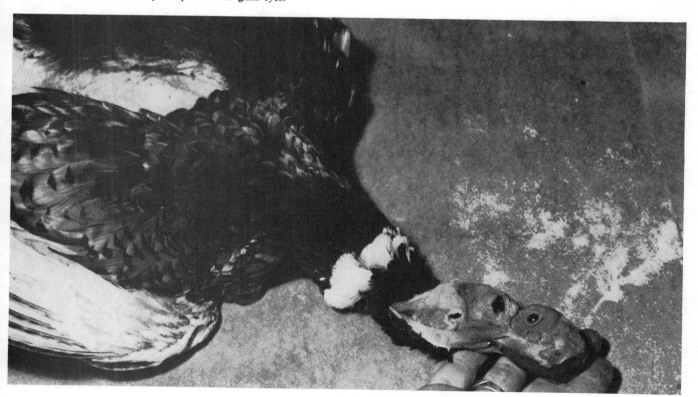

depends on the size of the bird. Get one of sufficient size to give overall balance to the finished mount. A similar perch can be improved from a larger limb, cutting the stump through the center, mounting the bird on the curved part in the desired position and using the flattened side to rest on a table *(illustration 4-23)*.

After drilling appropriate holes for the leg wires, put the wires through the holes and leave about an inch exposed beneath. Any excess can be trimmed off. Wrap the bare ends of the wires back against the perch to hold the bird snugly in place.

If any excess wire is exposed above the bird's head, push the head down slightly and clip off the wire level with the top of the head. Now the head can be pulled up, drawing the exposed end of wire into the brain cavity.

Now look at your mount critically. The entire bird can be moved around to give it a lifelike appearance and balance. Bend the wires very carefully to keep from ruining the mount. If you want the wings closed, push them in slowly, bending one joint at a time, until the feathers lie naturally when the wing is folded against the body. If you decide to leave the wings outspread *(illustration 4-24)*, get some heavy paper and cut four pieces about 2 to 3 inches in width (depending on the size of the bird) and as long as the wings. Put one strip on the top and one on the bottom of each wing and pin them together. These papers serve as braces to hold the feathers naturally as the mount dries; they prevent the feathers from warping and turning.

On a closed-wing mount, put paper braces on the longer feathers near the rear, and wrap the mount lightly with several turns of thread, to hold the feathers down, or use cardboard and secure against the feathers by sticking straight pins into the body *(illustration 4-25)*.

At this stage you should check the mount several times. Try to make it appear natural. It shouldn't look as if it were ready to topple off its perch. If the tail needs raising or lowering, do this by slowly bending the wires and repositioning the tail support wire. Cock the head in a natural position.

If you haven't already added the eyes, put them in place now. If they were positioned earlier, you may want to move them slightly before the clay dries. Adjust the eyelid to get the expression you want. Lids wide open give an expression of alertness; half-closed lids make the bird appear sleepy. Use your imagination to get an overall balance of head, wings, tail and eyes that makes the mount appear lifelike.

Put the mount in a cool, shady spot to dry for about 2 weeks.

Step 4 —*Finishing*

With a good grade of oil paint, paint the feet their natural color. You'll have to mix several different colors to get the exact shade. Paint the bill with clear varnish or clear fingernail polish to make it appear slick. If there

4-18. The wires of the wings are shoved completely through the form.

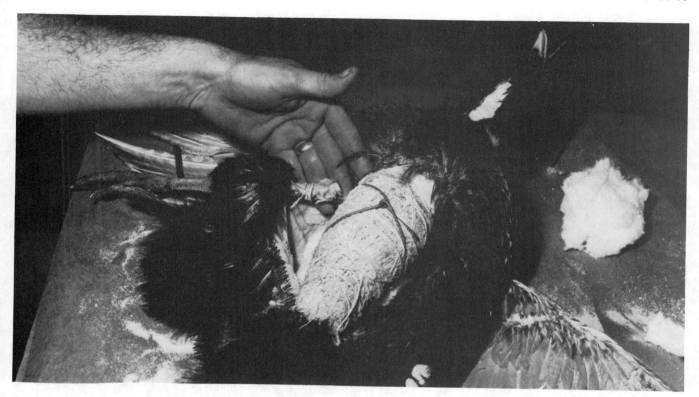

4-19. Two or three wraps of tied twine hold the leg bone to the wire.

4-20 Fill out the cavity with quilting cotton and sew up the bird.

4-21. A perch can be made by cutting a tree limb to this shape.

4-22. Stumps cut from limbs also make likely perches.

4-23. Cover the long feathers with cardboard and wrap the bird lightly with thread.

are no feathers on the bird's head, the head must be painted its natural color. Painting will also serve to preserve it.

As was stated earlier, all the steps except for the finishing can be accomplished at one sitting. But should you be short of time after skinning the bird, place the skin in the refrigerator until the next day. Don't try to hurry through the first three steps. In taxidermy, patience and quality are synonymous.

Combs and Wattles

A special problem is created by birds, such as turkeys (domestic or wide) or chickens, which have wattles, combs or both. If left alone, these parts which cannot be skinned will dry and shrink and look unnatural.

Some taxidermists recommend making molds of these parts, casting artificial wattles and combs, and putting them in place to substitute for the originals. For making molds of small parts such as this—or anything tiny you might need in any taxidermy procedure—you can use dental impression material, which is available at most drugstores. There are several kinds. Two that Lem Rathbone has used are Hydro-stone and Hydro-cal. Although made by the same company, the two have different densities, with Hydro-cal not being quite as

4-24. On an open-wing mount, cardboard strips should be placed top and bottom along each wing and also across tail feathers to hold them straight while the mount is drying.

hard. Probably the easiest to obtain, however, is white dental plaster. It is labeled 1-, 2-, 3- or 4-minute plaster, according to the time required for the mixed substance to set up or harden. If possible, buy 4-minute plaster; it gives you more time to work.

But rather than merely molding and casting the wattles and/or comb, Rathbone prefers to make a cast of the entire head. Cut off the bald head right where the feathers end on the neck. Position the wattles and comb naturally and place the head in the freezer.

While it is freezing, prepare to make a mold, as was described for a plastic fish in chapter 3. Take out the frozen head and hold it under running water briefly to rinse away the frost. Then half-bury the head in sand and cover it with No. 1 molding plaster. After this side hardens, turn it over, apply a separator around the edges, and cover the second side with plaster. You can use the separator described for plastic fish (chapter 3), but one that Rathbone likes even better is stearic acid, which you can get at a drugstore, mixed with an equal amount of kerosene. Despite its ominous-sounding name, stearic acid is not harmful.

Once the mold is hard, remove the head and tie the two halves together. Follow the procedure used to make the lifelike snake (chapter 14), pouring P-300 rubber compound into the mold.

When the head is cast it will be hollow and slightly flexible and can be used as is, except for adding eyes in the same way as for the lifelike snake.

To place the artificial head on the body, cut the neck portion to the right shape and sew the head into place. Later use wax to cover the stitches. When the mount is completed and dried, the head can be painted the correct colors.

4-25 Cardboard strips also can be used on closed-wing mounts, using straight pins to attach the strips. Run pins into the body to hold the wing feathers down, and on the tail put one strip above, one below, and hold them together with more pins.

5/Big-Game Head Mounts

5/Big-Game Head Mounts

As I look around my den, where I usually do my writing, I can relive some of my most exciting outdoor adventures. I look at the large black bass mounted in all its splendor and recall thrilling moments when I hooked it and brought it to net. Childhood memories return when I gaze at the mounted head of the first whitetail deer I ever killed. There is a mounted head of a huge mule deer, a memento of a Colorado hunt. Yet of all these, the one that gives me the greatest satisfaction is the mount of a large whitetail deer.

This mount is special to me for a couple of reasons. For one, it was the biggest whitetail I had ever killed up to that time, some 20 years ago. When I look at the mount I remember how I outwitted this particular monarch of the woods.

A friend and I were hunting in the brush and cactus country of South Texas, where whitetails run to record size in antlers if not in body. It was just after daybreak on a cold, still December morning and we were sitting on the slope of a small hill. My companion was banging two antlers together while I watched intently for any sign of movement that would suggest an approaching deer.

Many large bucks in South Texas are outwitted by the method of knocking a pair of antlers together to simulate the sounds of two bucks fighting. During the mating season bucks often fight for the affections of a female. When a buck hears two other bucks fighting, he is often attracted to the melee, hoping that he can lure the female away while the others are engaged in combat.

After about 30 minutes of watching and periodically hitting the antlers together, we suddenly noticed a deer approaching across the brushy valley below. His wide, heavy antlers caught the sunlight. I can recall how the crosshairs of the scope sight settled behind his shoulders and how he crashed into the cactus when I pulled the trigger.

Anyone who bags a very special animal wants to preserve it. Perhaps it is the first animal of its kind you have killed, or maybe it is a particularly large specimen. All of us like to show off our feats to others. And, besides, there is an additional satisfaction in looking at a mount which you have created yourself.

Mounting the head of a big-game animal isn't difficult. Mannequins are available at nominal prices and they do much to simplify the process. In addition to the challenge of mounting the animal yourself there is also the matter of economics. The average price of a professional mounting of a big-game head will run to almost $100, maybe more, depending on where you get the job done. You can do the mounting at home for about one-tenth of the commercial price.

The quality of your finished mount will depend greatly on how the animal is handled *before* you start mounting it. Never cut the throat of an animal you plan to mount. If the animal shows any sign of life, shoot it again. Any unnecessary cuts only compound the headaches of mounting. Large cuts are difficult to repair and almost impossible to keep from showing.

When field-dressing the animal, never cut entirely to the shoulders. Stop the incision this side of the shoulders. This will leave enough uncut skin for the cape, which is the part of the hide that will be required for the mount.

BIG-GAME HEAD MOUNTS
(Whitetail Deer)

TOOLS
Tape measure
Sharp knife
Screwdriver
Hammer
5-gallon container
Brush with stiff bristles
Large comb
Pliers
Drill with ¼-inch bit
Small paintbrush
Coping saw

SUPPLIES
10 pounds table salt or fine stock salt
1 pound alum
1 pound 20 Mule Team Borax
[Note: a dry or liquid preservative can be used instead of the pickling solution.]
Mannequin (to be ordered)
Glass eyes (to be ordered)
Ear liners (to be ordered)
25 No. 3 finishing nails
25 No. 2 shingle nails
Glover's needle
Nylon fishing line 6-pound test and 15-pound test
Wood screws
   2 1½-inch
   1 2-inch
Beeswax and turpentine
Black lacquer
1 pound potter's clay or fire clay
Piece of pine board 12 by 14 inches

Step 1 —*Measurements for Ordering Mannequin*

With a tape measure (cloth or flexible steel), get the animal's vital statistics *(illustration 5-1)*. These measurements are necessary in ordering a mannequin. In all, three measurements are required: 1) from tip of nose to front corner of eye (line *A* to *B*); 2) from tip of nose to back of head (line *A* to *C*); and 3) circumference of neck, measured just below the jawbone (line *D*). Make sure that the measurements are accurate. Do not attempt to make the mount larger than the animal actually was. The object is to re-create the animal as it was in life. Mannequins can be ordered from the supply sources listed in the appendix.

The mannequin should be roughly the same size as the head and neck with the hide off, but getting accurate measurements after you have skinned the animal can be a problem since some flesh will come off with the hide.

To provide the mannequin supplier with the best information available, take the outside measurements with the skin on and later take the same measurements inside after the skin has been taken off. Indicate which is which.

Without adding to the confusion, perhaps there should be a brief explanation as to what is involved here. No two big-game animals will have precisely the same measurements. For this reason any mannequin you order probably will require some alterations to fit your individual needs.

As is stressed in this and later chapters, it is easier to add to a mannequin than to take parts of it off. If the mannequin isn't quite large enough, you can increase the size by building up with clay or a papier-mâché-and-glue mix (see appendix). Attempting to trim the mannequin uniformly to reduce size is much more time-consuming and difficult, and the finished product won't be as good.

Alterations in a mannequin are not really that big a deal, as you will learn after you've attempted a few taxidermy jobs which demand the procedure.

Step 2 —*Skinning*

These instructions apply to whitetail deer, the most common big-game animal, but all animals of this size are similar. Three tools are needed: a sharp knife (one with about a 4-inch blade is best), a screwdriver at least 8 inches long and a saw (a meat saw is best, but an ordinary carpenter's saw will suffice). In the way of supplies you'll need about 2 pounds of table salt or fine stock salt.

When skinning the head for mounting, you can either skin the entire animal or skin only that part needed for the mount (the cape). If you skin the entire animal, hang

A mounted head can have a slight turn either to left or right.

If you prefer, the deer can be mounted looking straight ahead.

5-1. Three measurements are required when ordering a mannequin.

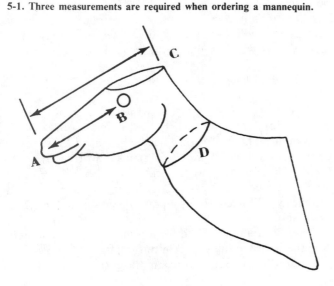

it by its hind legs, head down. After skinning as far as you can go down the neck, sever the neck. This lets you put the head on a table for skinning, which greatly simplifies the job.

Skinning the head requires time. Don't hurry. Allot yourself at least two hours.

The head should be skinned in such a way that everything comes off completely—ears, eyelids and part of the inner lip. When the cape is completely removed from the skull, it should be reasonably clean, with very little flesh still attached.

Begin by making a straight cut across the top of the head from one antler to the other. Use the screwdriver to pry the skin away from the antler bases *(illustration 5-2)*. If the skin doesn't separate easily, you may have to start it with the blade of your knife. Avoid tearing the

5-2. Cut between the antlers and separate the skin from the antlers with a screwdriver.

5-3. Another cut is made up the back of the cape,
bisecting the first cut.

skin or leaving any attached to the antler bases. With a horned animal, you'll have to cut the skin away from the bases with a knife. Remember that the horns must be boiled off their bases, the bases scraped clean, and the horns reseated with plaster of Paris (see chapter 3).

Once the skin is freed from the antler bases, make another incision the full length of the cape, up what would be the back. This cut should meet the one made across the top of the skull *(illustration 5-3)*. The perpendicular incision should be straight, through the cape, and not zigzagged.

Separate the cut, and skin the neck, turning the hide over the head as you approach the ears. When you reach the ear bases, cut the ears away from the skull, leaving the ears attached to the skin *(illustration 5-4)*. Continue skinning to the eyes. As you cut around the eyes, be particularly careful; the skin grows close to the skull here. The eyelids must be cut away from the skull so they remain on the hide. Eyelids are difficult to patch; avoid cutting them if possible. One method for getting a close cut is to put the index finger, (the one next to the thumb)

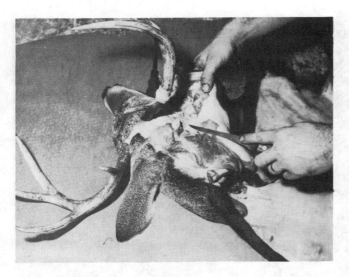

5-4. Cut under the base of the ear,
leaving the ear attached to the hide.

of the hand that is not holding the knife into the eye socket and push back as far as you can (illustration 5-5). By shoving the finger against the back of the socket, you can feel around the end as you cut. By doing this you can tell where the skin meets the socket. This also makes you cut more carefully: Should you get reckless with the knife, you may slice through the skin and into your finger.

Just below the eye there is a tear gland (illustration 5-6). Carefully separate the skin here with the end of your knife, or pry the skin loose from the skull with the screwdriver. Continue down to the mouth. Again, you can shove your finger deep into the mouth, where you can cut around the bulge created by the pressure of your finger against the skin (illustration 5-7). As you skin out the mouth, save as much of the lips as possible, as you'll need them in the mounting process. Finish separating the skin from the skull by skinning the nose. Avoid leaving too much flesh around the nose and lips. It will spoil and cause the hair to come loose.

At this stage the skin should have the ears, eyelids and part of the inner lips attached. Set the skull aside for the present.

The next step is to skin out the ears. Begin by skinning around the flesh that covers the cartilage where you separated the ear from the skull (illustration 5-8). Take care not to cut a hole on the bottom side of the ear where the opening comes down. Once you have skinned past the flesh there is only cartilage and skin. Upon reaching the cartilage, push your thumb between cartilage and skin and, applying pressure, separate the two to the ear end (illustration 5-9).

As you progress, turn the ear inside out. You may

have to employ the screwdriver as you approach the end, as the ear gets smaller. Make sure that you get completely to the end of the ear. Cut the cartilage where the ear ends, taking away the chunk of flesh on the end (illustration 5-10) and leaving the ear turned wrong side out (illustration 5-11). Follow the same procedure with the other ear. The ear is left with the hair inside so that the fleshy side can be salted.

Should any chunks of flesh be left clinging to the skin, trim these away with your knife. Now liberally coat the inside of the hide with table salt or fine stock salt. Rub the salt in well and be sure the entire hide is covered. Get the salt entirely to the edges, into the ears and around the lips and nose. Any spots that you miss will spoil. Roll the cape tightly, flesh side in, and put in a cool, dry spot to drain (the salt releases considerable moisture from the hide). The importance of this step cannot be overemphasized. If the hide is salted and cured properly, there will be no slippage of hair.

In about two days unroll the cape, give a second salt application, and roll again, putting it back in the cool place. With this preparation, the cape will keep for several weeks, or until you are ready to pickle it.

Next comes the skull. With the saw, make a horizon-

5-5. Stick your finger into the eye socket
and skin around the end of the finger.

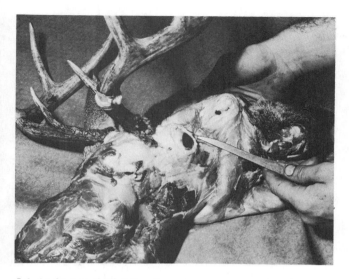

tal cut, starting just behind the antlers and cutting straight through, emerging about halfway up the nose *(illustration 5-12)*. Remove the brains and flesh from the skull plate that holds the antlers. Allow the skull to dry. The skull plate and the cape are all you need for a head mount.

Step 3 —*Ordering Necessary Supplies*

While the cape is curing and pickling, you can order the mannequin, two glass eyes and two ear liners. A mannequin is the greatest bargain in taxidermy. For a few dollars you are buying a professional's skill. After a mold is made, a person with the know-how can turn out thousands of mannequins. But making a mold is expensive, and unless you expect to assembly-line at least several hundred mannequins, the effort is not worth the

5-6. At the tear gland, below the eye, the skin grows close to the skull.

5-7. Stick your finger into the mouth and cut around the end of the finger.

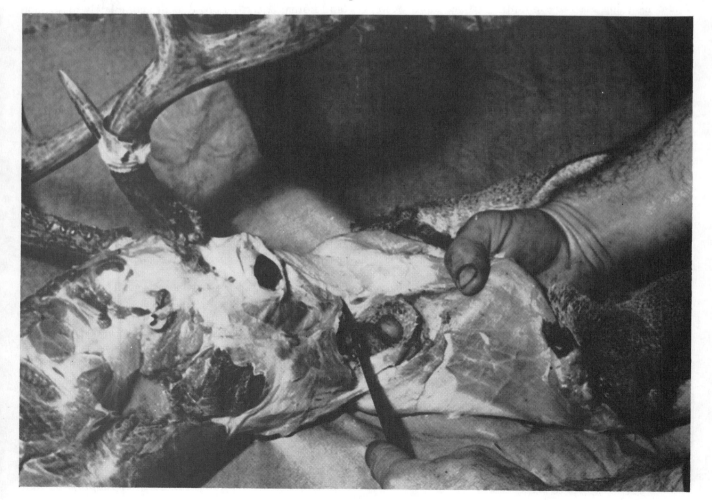

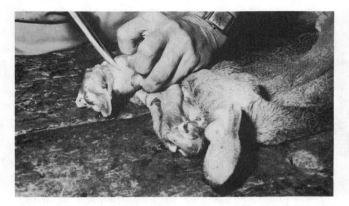

5-8. Skin the base of the ear until you come to the cartilage.

5-10. Cut away the chunk of flesh at the base of the ear.

time and expense. Be sure to give your supplier all the measurements of the deer; without these he cannot determine what size mannequin you need. Also specify whether you want a mannequin facing head-on, or turned either left or right.

Sculpturing a mannequin is the most complex and time-consuming step in mounting a big-game head. When you purchase the mannequin you greatly simplify your task.

Step 4—*Preserving the Cape*

For preserving the cape, use a dry or liquid quick preservative, or the pickling solution with this job. The quick preservative tends to be less messy; on the other hand, pickling has long proved that it can preserve a deer cape indefinitely. The deer I mounted is still in excellent condition after more than 20 years.

For pickling, you will need 8 pounds of salt, 1 pound of alum and 1 pound of 20 Mule Team Borax, plus a container that holds at least 5 gallons of liquid, preferably

a plastic trash can or wash tub. A tin container will rust if used more than once.

Clean the container and pour 3 gallons of water into it. Take another container—an ordinary kitchen pot or pan will do—and pour in 1 gallon of water and bring it to a boil. When the water is boiling, add the salt, alum and borax. After the powders are completely dissolved, pour the mixture into the 3 gallons of water and allow all 4 gallons to cool completely. Now entirely submerge the cape in the liquid. Agitate the hide briskly so that every bit of it is saturated. Allow the hide to pickle for at least a week, agitating it every other day. Heavier hides, such as those of moose and elk, require more pickling time, 10 days to 2 weeks. If necessary, the pickle can be left with the hide in it for a month or longer, until you are ready to work with it.

Step 5 —*Attaching Antlers to Mannequin*

For attaching the skull and antlers to the mannequin, on the wall or a similar support, put two hangers (nails),

5-9. Use your thumb to separate the cartilage from the skin.

5-11. This is the way the ear looks when it is turned.

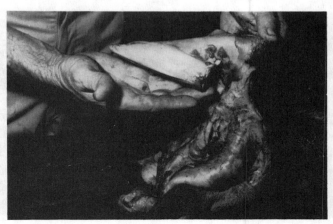

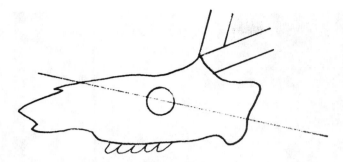

5-12. Remove the skull plate by sawing from behind antlers through eye socket to nose.

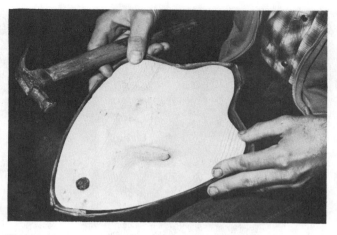

5-13. A piece of board is cut and nailed into the base of the mannequin. A urethane form will come supplied with the back board in place.

one about knee-level (for working on the back of head) and another about chest-high (for working on the mouth and nose). Trace the back of the mannequin on a piece of pine board, and using a coping saw, cut this out, slightly smaller than the pattern so that it will fit on the back of the mannequin. Put the board in place and anchor it with nails around the edges *(illustration 5-13)*. Drill a hole in the board, and use this to hang the mannequin on the wall nails.

Start by hanging the mannequin on the knee-high hanger. Position the skull plate on top of the mannequin, matching the eye sockets in the skull to the eye sockets in the mannequin. You may have to saw more bone off the skull plate to make it fit snugly; if it is out of level, you might have to use small wedges of wood to make it sit straight. Drill two one-quarter inch holes forward of the antlers, in the front part of the skull plate, about 2 inches from the edge, and another single hole behind the antlers, centered in the back of the skull. The two 1½-inch wood screws go into the forward holes; the 2-inch screw fits through the back hole. These screws anchor the skull plate to a block of wood built into the mannequin.

Tighten the three screws lightly. Place the mannequin on the high hanger and step back and study it. Do the antlers appear natural? If not, loosen the screws, remove more bone or add wedges of wood, retighten screws, and check the alignment of the antlers again. When you are satisfied that they look natural, as if they were on a live deer, proceed with the contouring of the top part of the head. Using clay (or plaster of Paris if you prefer), fill in around the skull plate, modeling over the crack between skull plate and mannequin, and contour the top of the skull plate naturally, substituting clay for the flesh you removed earlier. Just be careful not to overdo it. While this sculpturing *(illustration 5-14)* is done now, the modeling of the facial structure is not to be done until you are actually ready to put the cape on the mannequin. This is because the clay around the eyes, nose and mouth must be fresh and moist when you put the cape

on the mannequin, so that these features can be modeled naturally.

Step 6 —*Cleaning the Cape*

Allow yourself at least 5 hours for this step. Remove the hide from the pickling solution, lay it flat, flesh side up, on a table, and with a sharp knife scrape the fleshy side thoroughly, to remove and rough up the membrane. Then cut the lips down thin, shaving away all the flesh on the inside of the hide, so that the hide will mold to the mannequin smoothly. Pay special attention to the eye

5-14. Clay or plaster of Paris is used to model around the attached skull plate.

5-15. Trim away the excess flesh around the eyes, nose and mouth.

and nose areas. All the flesh must be removed. A handy accessory is a piece of 4-inch-wide board tapered to a point; this permits you to hold the cape snugly as you shave it *(illustration 5-15)*. (See chapter 13, Tanning, for details on making a fleshing board.) Should you run out of time during this operation, submerge the cape in the pickle again and return to it later.

If there are any holes, sew them shut. With a bullet hole, remove some hide, cutting an elongated football-shaped pattern around it *(illustration 5-16)*. This permits you to pull the cut together so that the edges match and lie flat. Never hesitate to cut the hole larger; often this is necessary to repair the cut. Use a glover's three-edged needle and ordinary 6-pound-test nylon fishing line. This same test nylon is sufficient for sewing up the mouth and ears, but about 15-pound test is needed to close the incision down the back of the cape.

Sew the mouth so that the two edges of hair just come

5-16. Cut a football-shaped piece from around a bullet hole to allow the leather to lie flat.

together. The nostrils and ear passages will be taken care of later. When the mouth is sewed and any holes are repaired, put the cape back in the pickling solution.

Step 7 —*Mounting*

When you are ready to model the facial structure, take the cape out of the pickling solution and place it in water with powdered detergent added, to allow it to soak and remove the pickle.

Take about a cup of potter's clay or fire clay and mix with water. The consistency should be about like modeling clay. If you get it too wet, add more dry mix.

Put a small amount of clay into the eye sockets and push the glass eyes into the clay. Look at them critically to make sure they are straight. Shove the eyes well in; otherwise the mount will appear bug-eyed. After you have the eyes positioned to suit you, add a small amount of clay along the brow ridge and some around the eyes to hold them snugly, and also to model the raised muscles found over the eyes of deer. Put more clay around the mouth and nostrils, modeling the head so that it appears natural. The tendency is to use too much clay rather than too little. Only a small amount is needed to anchor the mouth, nose and ears to the mannequin *(illustration 5-17)*. Wet your hand in water from time to time while smoothing the clay.

5-17. Clay is used to model the brow ridge, and around the eyes, mouth and nose.

Remove the cape from the soapy water and rinse it thoroughly in clear water. After rinsing, it should be thoroughly saturated, slick and stretchy. Let it drain a few minutes, to remove any excess water, and slip the ear liners into place *(illustration 5-18)*. If the liners are too large, trim the edges slightly with your knife. Sew with the 6-pound-test fishing twine up the middle of the ear, taking about one-half inch stitches from base to tip. This holds the ear and liner together while the mount is drying. If the stitching shows in the finished mount, it can be removed later.

Now place the cape on the mannequin, pulling the hide up to the antlers, and, using ordinary nails, anchor the skin near the antlers to hold it in position. Any small nails will do; drive them in just far enough to hold the hide. Later they will be removed. Place the eye holes over the glass eyes and position the nose properly. Force the lips into the clay, pushing with a screwdriver against the seam where you sewed the two lips together. Try to make the mouth look as natural as possible. Push the nostrils into the nose of the mannequin. Add a No. 3 finishing nail on each side of the nose to hold the nostrils permanently in place.

Put a No. 3 finishing nail at each corner of the eyes, driving the nails completely in. Open the eyes just slightly less than you want them to be in the finished mount as they will open some as they dry. Use a knife or screwdriver to model around the eyes until they appear natural *(illustration 5-19)*.

Now take the 15-pound-test fishing twine and glover's needle and, pulling the hide snugly around an antler base, start sewing the top incision closed. The hide must be very tight around the base as it tends to pull away as the mount dries. Place stitches about one-quarter inch apart, sewing to the center of the T-cut, or where the cut up the back of the cape intercepts the cut made between the two antlers. Now take another piece of twine and start at the opposite antler and sew to the middle again, bringing the two stitch jobs together. Tie the thread ends together where they meet. Continue to sew down the back of the neck *(illustration 5-20)*. Here you may have to employ pliers to pull the skin around, bringing both sides of the incision together. When you finish sewing, tie the thread securely. Using No. 2 shingle nails, nail the loose or excess skin to the back board, spacing nails about 1 inch apart. Be sure the hide is pulled snugly and

5-18. Ear liners are slipped into the hide.

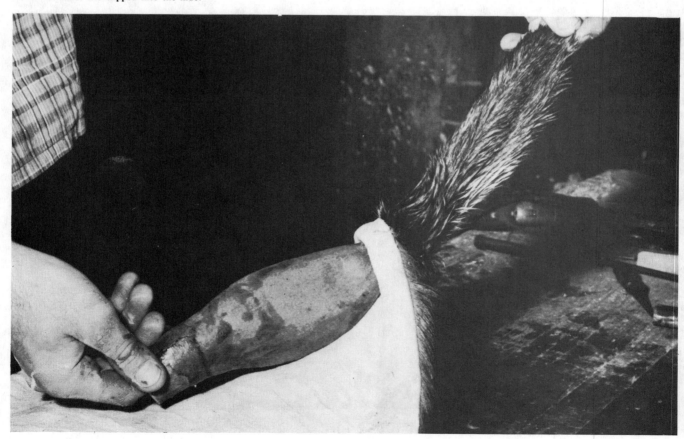

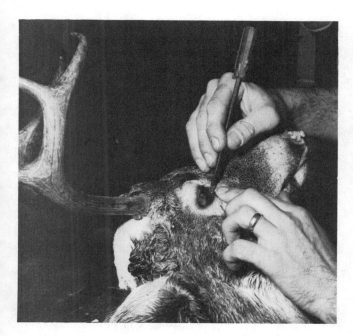

5-19. Model the eyes naturally with a screwdriver or similar tool.

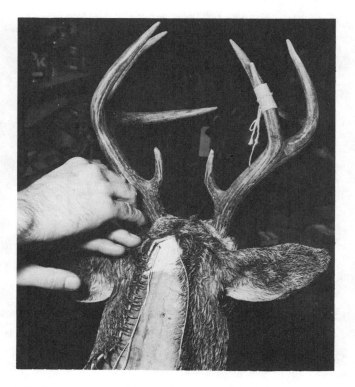

smoothly entirely around the base of the mannequin. Remove the temporary nails around the antlers and brush and comb the hair exactly as you want it.

Mix about one-quarter cup of clay. Roll the clay into small balls and pack these in the ears, ramming the clay down against the mannequin. Move the ears around until you find their natural position. Use enough clay to fill up the bases so that the ears will stand up. Put two or three No. 3 finishing nails under each ear and enough nails down the brisket to hold the hide in place. Tack around the face wherever additional anchoring is needed. These nails are permanent; drive them in completely. The hair will hide them.

Step 8 —*Finishing*

Allow the mount to dry for at least 2 weeks in ordinary weather, longer under humid conditions. After it is totally dried, take a small amount of beeswax and mix it with turpentine to a consistency about like modeling clay. Put some around the eyes, using the sharp end of a knife or a screwdriver to fill the crack between the glass eye and the hide completely *(illustration 5-21)*. Add some more inside of nostril holes, using only enough to fill up the cracks at skin edge. Now using a small paintbrush and black lacquer, paint the end of the nose lightly in the nostrils and around the eyes. Brush the mount with a stiff-bristled brush, to make the hair loose and more lifelike.

5-20. Sew the top cut first, then sew down the back of the cape.

5-21. Use beeswax to fill in around the eyes, mouth and nostrils.

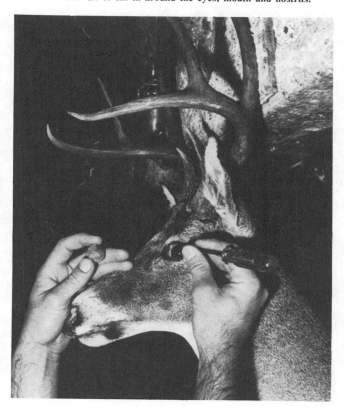

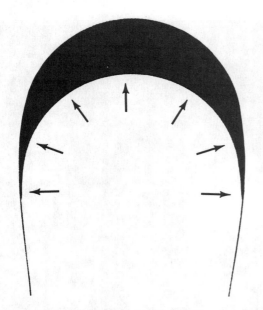

5-22. Lips should be opened to the end where they will fold flat for shaving.

5-23. Cut two slits in mannequin, one on either side of mouth.

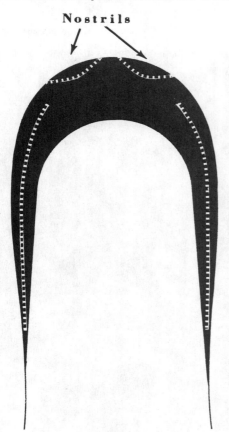

Alternate Method for Modeling Mouth

While sewing the mouth shut is by far the easiest method, it is not the best. As you progress in taxidermy, you'll undoubtedly want to use more advanced methods which will result in better work. This method, while a bit more complex, certainly makes the facial structure of the animal appear more natural.

Step 1 —*Skinning and Cleaning Cape*

When skinning the head, be sure that you leave as much of the inner lips as possible, both on the lower and upper jaw. Later, when cleaning the cape, the lips must be separated from the hide, but not severed. Look at the mouth and you'll be able to distinguish the lips. Cutting from the inside out *(illustration 5-22)*, go under the lip with a sharp knife blade, cutting as close to the edge as possible. When you have finished you should be able to lay the lip out flat, bending it over, and you can shave the lip down thin.

Step 2 —*Preparing the Mannequin*

As you prepare the mannequin for mounting, take your knife and cut two slits in the form, one on each side of the mouth *(illustration 5-23)*. The slits do not need to

5-24. The slits are on both sides; the mouth doesn't have to be cut entirely around.

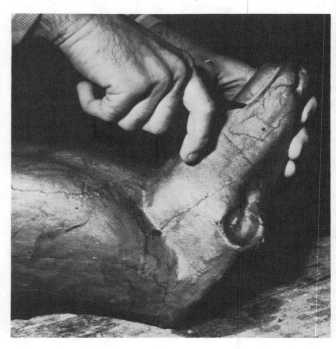

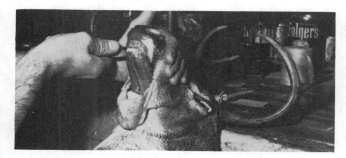

5-25. With a blunt instrument push the lips of the upper jaw into the mannequin.

5-26. Pull the lower lip over the upper lip and attach with No. 2 fine nails.

be completely around the mouth, only along each side *(illustration 5-24).*

Step 3—*Mounting*

Once the cape is placed on the mannequin, take a tapered instrument (a kitchen knife makes a good tool) and push the lips of the upper jaw into the slits *(illustration 5-25).* Now bring the lower lip up over the upper lip and anchor it with about five small nails *(illustration 5-26),* driving the nails in completely. With the tapered instrument, push the lips of the lower jaw into the same slits where you put the lips of the upper jaw. Push the lips far enough into the slits to make the mouth appear natural. In finishing, a small bit of beeswax along the

seam of the lips will obscure the nails.

Using a Plaque

The mount can simply be hung from a hook in the hole in the base of the mannequin but a plaque adds an extra touch. Plaques can be ordered from any of the supply sources listed in the appendix, or you can improvise your own *(illustration 5-27).* Stain the plaque to the desired color, allow it to dry, then position the mount on the plaque and, from the rear, drill three holes through the plaque in a triangle pattern. Use 2-inch wood screws in these holes to anchor the plaque to the mannequin base. A screw eye can be added to the top of the plaque for hanging the mount.

5-27. A plaque of your own design can be used for hanging the completed mount. The plaque on the left is unfinished; the one on the right with the hanger is finished.

6/Mounting a Whole Animal

6/Mounting a Whole Animal

The possibilities for mounting whole animals, life-sized, are almost unlimited. The fundamentals are the same for a small animal, like a squirrel, or a large one, such as a deer. When you order supplies from any of the supply sources listed in the appendix, ask for a catalog. You'll be amazed at the number of mannequins available for almost any conceivable animal. For larger animals, however, the prices are higher.

Neither the appendix to this book nor most commercial catalogs mentions rabbits. The cottontail rabbit, although abundant, is one of the most difficult of all animals to mount. Even professional taxidermists are reluctant to mount rabbits. But another small animal of widespread range, the squirrel, is quite easy to mount, and the basic mannequin is not very expensive. For a deer the price is pretty steep; the actual cost depends on the size of the animal. It is obvious, therefore, why I suggest starting with a small animal. After you have gained some skill, you may want to try a raccoon or a bobcat. But for now let's stick with the squirrel. If the squirrel mount isn't up to your expectations, write it off as experience. Learning hasn't been expensive.

Step 1 —Ordering the Mannequin

Once you obtain a specimen and the necessary supplies you can mount the animal in a day's time. If you already have the squirrel, freeze it whole, innards intact, until you have the necessary equipment, supplies, and time to mount it. Otherwise, get the mannequin and glass eyes; then obtain the specimen. When you order, specify the species of squirrel (gray or fox). See the appendix for the size of the glass eyes.

Two different types of mannequins are available. The basic mannequin is composed of the head and body, with wires for legs and tail. The more complete mannequin, with modeled feet, legs and more minute detail, costs quite a bit more. The basic mount is adequate for learning, but the more complete one results in a better finished product.

Step 2 —Skinning

Place some newspapers or an old sheet on a table and spread the squirrel on its stomach, feet outstretched. Make an incision from between the ears, along the back, to the base of the tail (illustration 6-1). Peel the hide down both sides (illustration 6-2). When you reach the tail, strip out the tail bone, being careful not to tear the skin. Now make another cut the full length of the tail (illustration 6-3). This cut can be made either along the top of the tail or underneath. If the tail is to be curved over the back, cut it along the top. The stitching then will be least noticeable. If the tail is to be extended straight back, make the cut underneath where it is more effectively hidden. After opening the tail completely, to the tip, rub the inside thoroughly with borax.

Proceed to the feet, skinning each leg down and over the foot and down each toe to the claw; clip here and leave the claw attached to the hide (illustration 6-4). When you have the four feet disengaged, go to the head and skin it out, peeling the hide over the skull and using the tip of your knife to cut between the hide and skull

(illustration 6-5). Avoid pulling so hard that the hide will tear. Pay particular attention to separating the ears from the skull, leaving them attached to the hide, and working carefully around the eyes, mouth and nose.

Open the hide and trim away any excess flesh. The head and nose will probably require the most attention (illustration 6-6). Sew the mouth shut, pulling the lips evenly together, and then wash the hide thoroughly in cool water with powdered detergent. After draining the hide, go over the entire flesh side liberally with borax, rubbing it vigorously into each crease. Roll the hide and

6-1. An incision is made the full length of the squirrel's back.

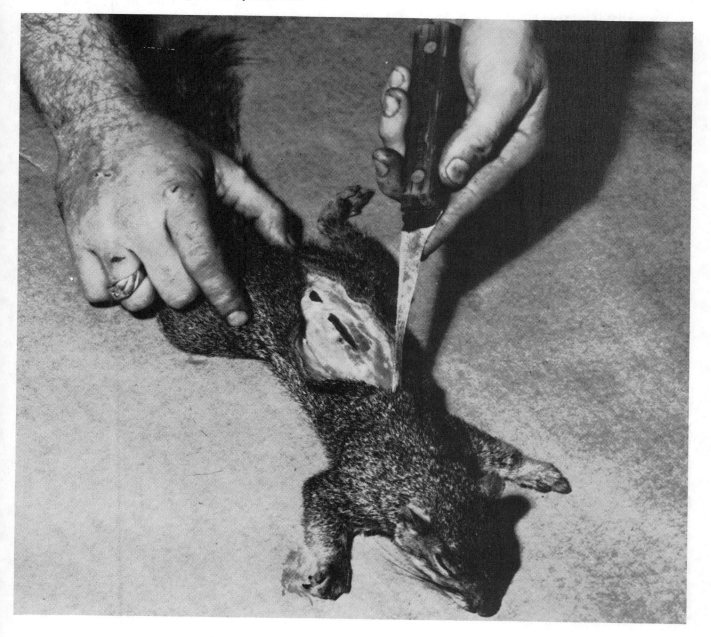

LIFE-SIZED MOUNTS
(Squirrel)

TOOLS
Sharp knife
Wire cutters
Brush
Drill with ¼-inch bit

SUPPLIES
Mannequin (to be ordered)
Glass eyes (to be ordered)
Ordinary heavy-duty sewing needle
Nylon fishing line 6-pound-test
¼ pound potter's clay or fire clay
Cotton
Mounting board
20 Mule Team Borax
[Note: a dry or liquid quick preservative can be substituted for Borax.]
Straight pins
Beeswax

put it under refrigeration until you have finished preparing the mannequin.

Step 3 —*Preparing the Mannequin*

Place a small amount of clay in the eye sockets of the mannequin and position the eyes. Make them look straight ahead and parallel with the nose. Put a minimal amount of clay around the mouth and nose, modeling as best you can the general shape and contour of a squirrel's head *(illustration 6-7).* Wrap a small amount of cotton around the wire for the tail, making it smooth and free of lumps. The cotton should extend only about half the length of the full tail *(illustration 6-8).* The tendency of most beginners is to get the tail oversized. Keep it small, about the size of an ordinary pencil at the base and tapered to the point. Wrap the cotton snugly with string to hold it in place.

Step 4 —*Mounting*

If you are using the basic mount without modeled feet, push enough clay into the skin of each leg to fill out the toes, feet and forelegs *(illustration 6-9);* with the more detailed mannequin, only a small amount of clay to fill the toes is required.

6-2. The hide is peeled both ways, exposing the body.

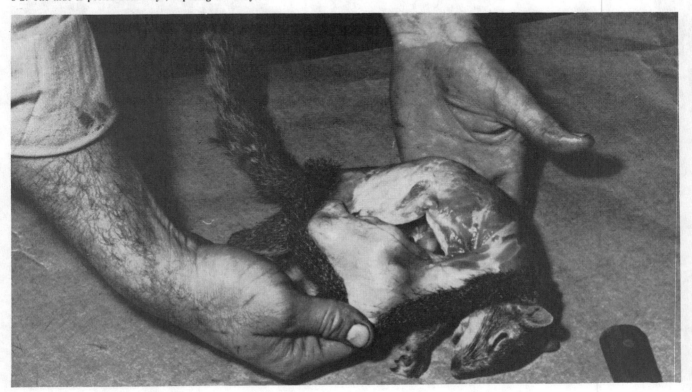

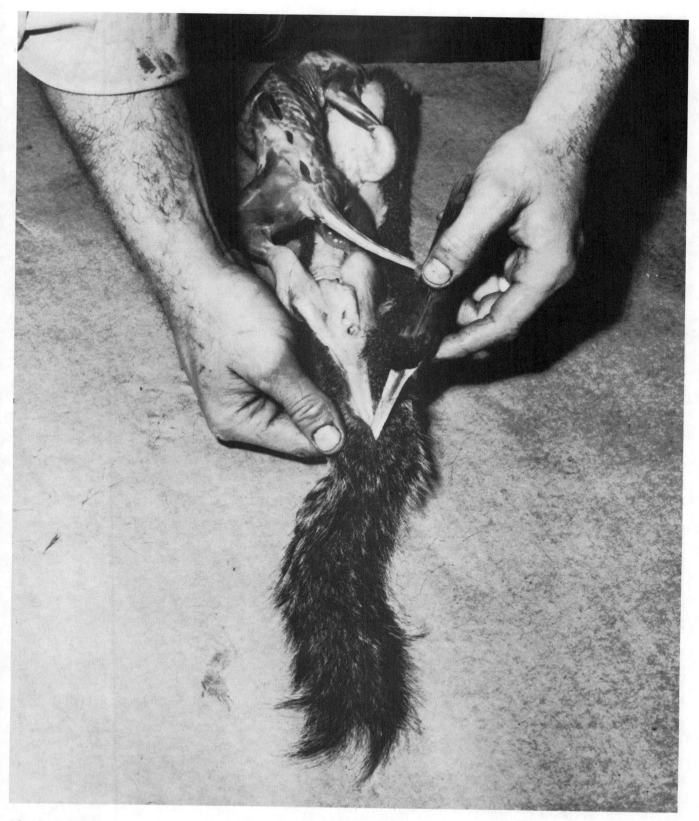

6-3. After stripping out the tail bone, a slit is made in the skin, full length.

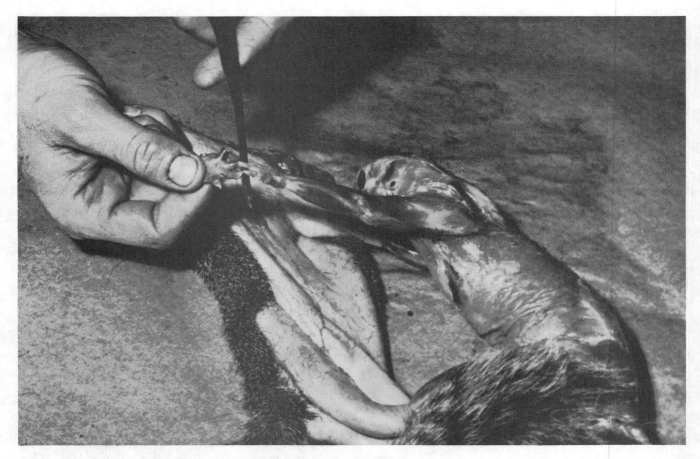

6-4. The feet are skinned to the claws, then clipped with a knife blade.

6-5. Use the point of a knife to skin out the head.

Now slip the skin onto the mannequin. Begin with the feet, pushing on the hide just as you would pull on trousers *(illustration 6-10)*. Thrust the wire on each foot down to the end of the foot and make a tiny hole in the bottom of the foot where the wire can exit. Pull the skin over the body, making sure you have it well up and in proper position. It is possible to stretch the skin and make the legs too long, creating a finished mount that is out of proportion. Bring the skin up and around the nose and over the head. Be sure the skin on the head is positioned naturally. Pull the incision together along the back and begin sewing, starting between the ears and sewing back *(illustration 6-11)*. An ordinary heavy-duty sewing needle and heavy sewing thread will suffice, but 6-pound-test nylon fishing line will give you a more durable mount, less susceptible to breakage. On a larger animal, you need a glover's needle and at least 6-pound-test nylon line. A raccoon, for example, has very tough hide.

As you sew the head in place, the ears of a squirrel will stand upright naturally, but on larger animals, such as a raccoon or bobcat, the ears must be skinned out, filled with some sort of cardboard liner and anchored to the skull with clay, as with the big-game head mount.

Make your stitches about one-eighth inch apart. As you get to the base of the tail, insert the cotton-rolled wire and sew to the tip of the tail.

Now anchor the squirrel to some sort of stand, either permanent or temporary. This permits you to work on it with both hands. Almost any kind of stand will do: a piece of board, a plaque, a stumplike chunk of limb or a limb that stands out from the wall like that used in mounting a bird.

Decide what position you wish the finished mount to assume. If the squirrel is to be squatting *(illustration 6-12)*, drill two holes in the board; determine about where these holes will be so the squirrel will be sitting naturally, not spraddle-legged (the width will vary with different squirrels). Run the hind-leg wires through the board and bend them underneath to secure the squirrel. If the squirrel is to be on all fours, drill four holes for the four leg wires.

If the squirrel is squatting, you may want to have it nibbling a nut. To accomplish this, drill shallow holes on either side of the nut: the holes should be opposite each other. Snip off the wires extending from the front feet, leaving about one-quarter inch of wire exposed on each. Bend each wire at right angles, inward, and push

6-6. All excess flesh around the lips, eyes and nose must be removed.

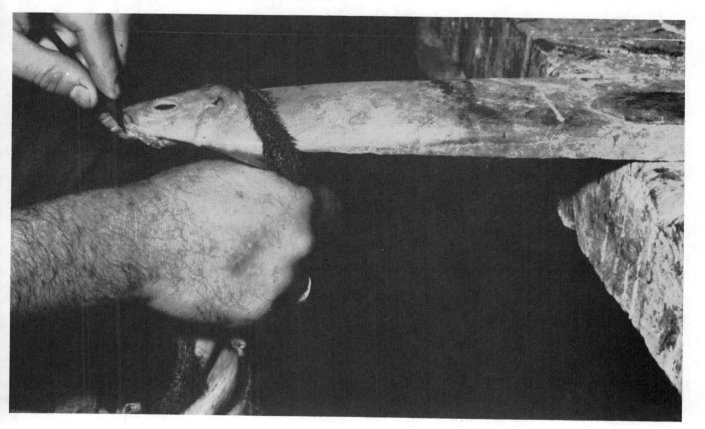

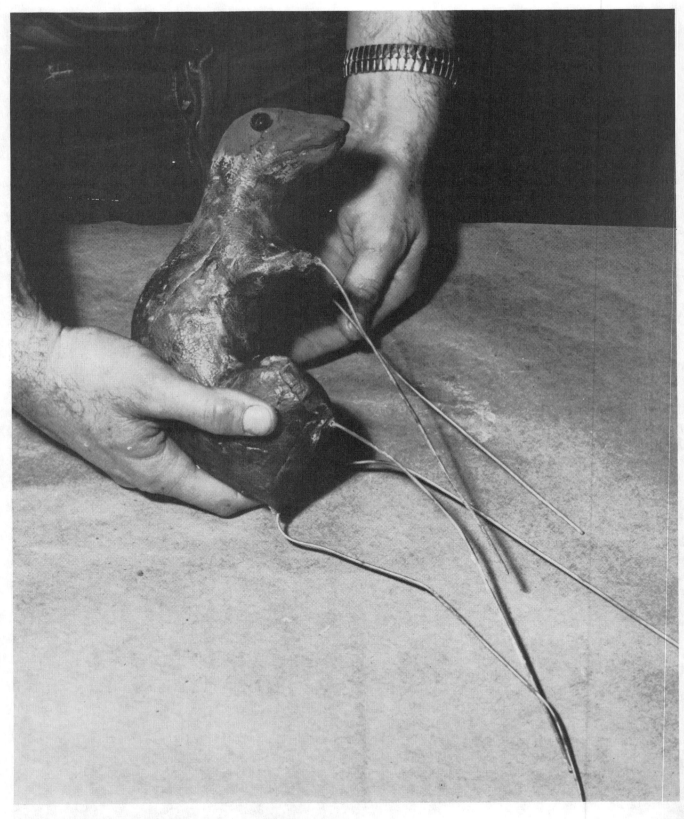

6-7. The head is modeled with clay and the glass eyes positioned.

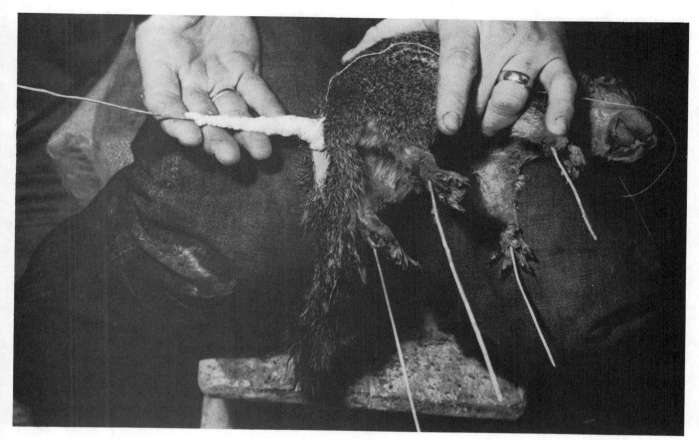

6-8. A small amount of cotton is wrapped on the tail wire.

6-9. Clay is pushed into the legs, to fill toes, feet and forelegs.

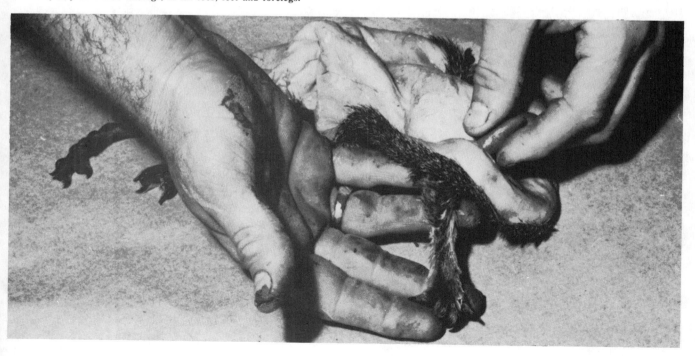

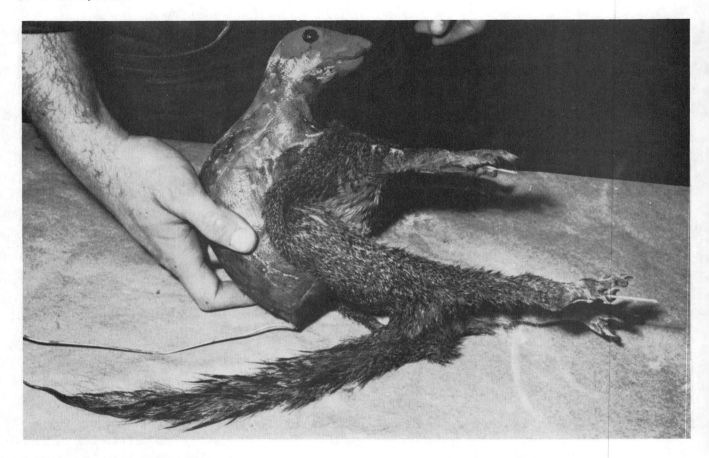

6-10. All four legs are slipped into place.

6-11. After the hide is pulled into place, sew it together from front to back.

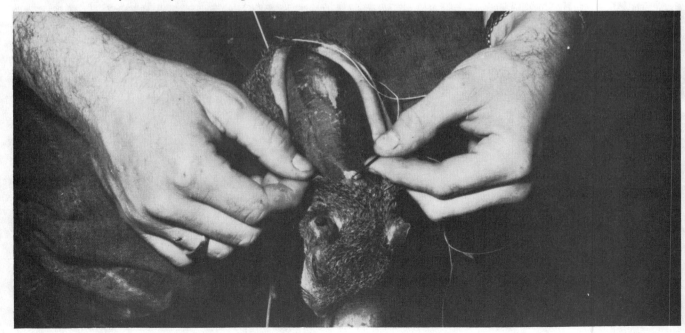

6-12. Put the squirrel on a perch and bend it into the desired position.

6-13. A pointed object is used to model the mouth, nose and eyes.

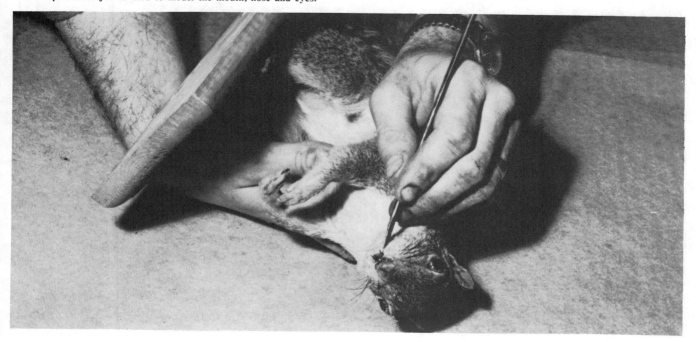

6-14. All sorts of mannequins for whole animals are available; this one is for a squatting gray fox.

the feet together, positioning the wires into the holes drilled in the nut. Curl the tail up over the squirrel's back.

Brush the mount vigorously, until the hairs are laying naturally. With a blunt or tapered instrument (the back of a knife blade will do), model the mouth, pushing it into the clay *(illustration 6-13)*. Stick a straight pin at each side of the mouth to hold it in place while the mount dries.

Pull the eyes into position and with straight pins, one forward and one back of each eye, anchor the skin until the mount dries. Later all the pins will be removed. Model around the eyes with your knife blade until they look natural.

Step 5 —*Finishing*

Allow the mount to dry completely. This will take about 2 weeks; the length of time will vary with weather conditions. Remove the pins, then take a small amount

6-15. The basic plan for squirrels applies to larger animals, like this raccoon.

6-16. A different touch, such as an upraised foot, can make a mount appear more lifelike.

6-17. Rathbone made this coyote seem more realistic by putting a mounted quail in its mouth.

of beeswax and model around the eyes, filling the creases to make the eyes appear alive. Remove any ex- cess clay that might be clinging to the eyes or skin. Comb the mount and it is ready for display.

7/Fish—Medium Size

7/Fish–Medium Size

For your first fish to mount pick one with scales, medium-sized; a specimen weighing about 3 pounds is ideal. Small fish and excessively large ones compound your problems; avoid these until you have had some practice. A scaled fish is easiest to mount.

This chapter deals with a largemouth black bass, perhaps the most widespread and common of all gamefish. But, basically, all fish are much the same. Some are more difficult, but the fundamentals are not too different. Taxidermist Rathbone remembers an Arctic grayling he once received for mounting. After making a mold of the fish (a precautionary measure he follows on a fish he's never worked with), he attempted to skin the delicate specimen. It practically disintegrated. Using the mold, he reconstructed the fish almost entirely, using liquid rubber to make an artificial skin and rebuilding the tail and fins from other materials. Very little of the actual fish was used, yet the customer was well pleased with the finished product.

A black bass is fairly simple to skin and work with, and in most parts of the United States, as well as adjoining countries, it is readily available as a specimen.

Step 1 —*Obtaining a Color Guide*

If possible, take several color photographs of the fish while it is fresh, preferably immediately after it is caught. These will serve as an invaluable guide when you are painting the mount. An alternative is to obtain a colorplate of a bass from a book or magazine. But markings vary from fish to fish, and it is best to have a photograph of the fish you are actually working with in order to make the completed mount as realistic as possible.

Step 2 —*Making a Pattern*

Examine the fish and choose its "show" side—the one which will be exposed. Often a fish will have a rubbed place or a cut on one side. Pick the one with the least damage to work with.

Take a piece of heavy paper slightly larger than the fish, place the specimen with its "show" side down on the paper, and with a pencil trace around it, to create a silhouette *(illustration 7-1)*. You may also want to make a plaster mold of the fish (see chapter 3). Such aids as a paper pattern and a mold are invaluable, both for determining the size of the mannequin needed and for getting the correct flow of lines so that the fish will look natural. When tracing the fish, it is imperative that you get its exact size; if you exaggerate it, the body won't fit inside the skin when you are mounting it.

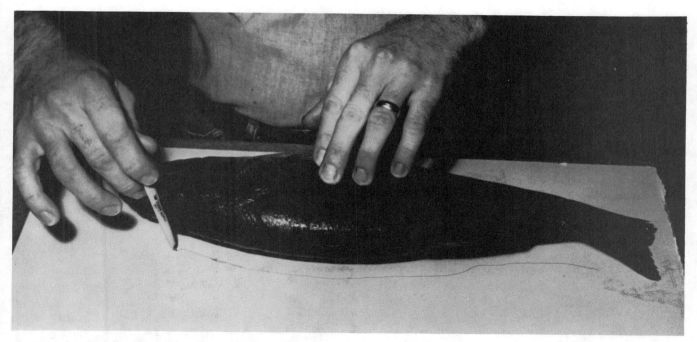

7-1. Trace around the fish on heavy paper to create a pattern.

Step 3 —*Skinning*

Now spread out an old sheet or similar large piece of old cloth and put the fish on it, "show" side down. Cloth is better than newspaper because the paper tends to get wet and stick to the fish and tear. Be sure that the fish is moist and remains damp as you work with it. Have a container of water handy and rub some over the fish every few minutes. Always keep the fins and tail wet, to prevent cracking and breaking. If you are working in a dry climate or a heated room, you might wrap the tail and fins with moist cotton to prevent drying.

Make an incision the full length of the fish, down the middle, from tail to gills. Commence skinning, using your knife to separate the skin from the flesh *(illustration 7-2)*. As you peel the skin back *(illustration 7-3)*, the first fin you encounter is the dorsal fin, on the fish's back. With tin snips or scissors, clip this fin at the base, leaving the fin attached to the skin *(illustration 7-4)*. Do the same with the anal fins (near the tail) and pectoral fins (near the gills) as you come to them. Skin toward the tail until you reach the end of the flesh; then cut the spine to dissect the tail from the body, leaving the tail attached to the skin *(illustration 7-5)*. If you are in doubt as to how far back to skin, leave some flesh clinging to the base of the tail; this flesh can be removed later. If you attempt to skin too far, you may bend or damage the skin so that it is almost impossible to repair.

Now with the snips or scissors—on large fish you may have to use wire cutters—clip the bone behind the gill

---

FISH—MEDIUM SIZE
(Black Bass, 5 Pounds or Smaller)

TOOLS
Sharp knife
Heavy-duty scissors or tin snips
Coping saw
Tablespoon
Screwdriver
Hammer

SUPPLIES
25 No. 2 fine nails
Balsa wood or mannequin
Glass eye
Potter's clay or fire clay
1 pound box 20 Mule Team Borax
3 or 4 small paintbrushes
Plaque
2 2-inch wood screws
2 screw eyes
Sandpaper
Cardboard
Straight pins
Bobby pins

7-2. **Make an incision the length of the fish, tail to gills, and commence skinning.**

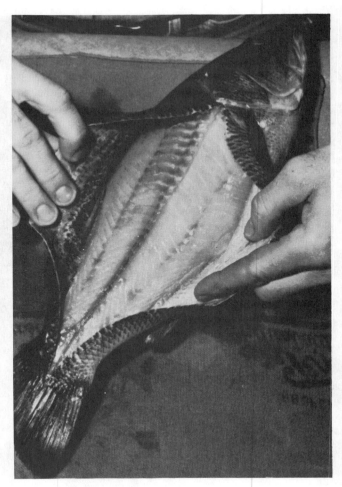

7-3. **Peel the skin back both ways until you encounter the fins.**

(illustration 7-6). Bend the bone both ways to open the skin, and skin each way as far as you can; then bend the body up sharply to separate the head from the body. The head remains attached to the skin *(illustration 7-7).*

Any flesh remaining on the skin can be scraped away, using the rounded end of a tablespoon or teaspoon *(illustration 7-8).* Clean out the skull completely, removing all surplus flesh, the eyes and tongue and gills. There is a lot of bone structure in the head and as much of this as possible should be eliminated. If the scissors or snips are too bulky and awkward to use, you may have to employ small wire cutters. About the only way bone can be removed is by clipping. Some bone must be removed so that you can get into the brain cavity to remove the brains. When you are finished, the skin should be almost entirely free of flesh and bone *(illustration 7-9).*

Wash the skin in cool water with powdered detergent, getting it very clean. Rinse it thoroughly and allow it to drain, then roll it in a wet towel and place it in the refrigerator while you construct the mannequin. Keep the fish's body as a guide in making the mannequin.

Step 4 —*Preparing the Mannequin*

A urethane form or mannequin can be ordered from any taxidermy supply house (see Appendix). Specify the species and include measurements for total length of the fish and its girth. While it is acceptable to make a form for medium-sized fish, such as the bass we are working with in this chapter, a commercial form is recommended for fish weighing 5 pounds or more. But be sure to wrap the fish in a wet towel and put it in the freezer until the mannequin arrives and you are ready to go to work.

For those who make their own forms, Louis Keller, a custom fish taxidermist, recommends that they be carved from soft wood. Avoid any of those white blocks of foam plastic; they tend to lack rigidity, break too easily, and are difficult to shape. Balsa wood is the best, but you

7-4. Use tin snips to clip the fin bases from the body.

7-5. Sever the body just forward of the tail.

7-6. Clip the heavy bone at the base of the gill.

7-7. The body should be broken from the skin and retained as a guide in constructing the mannequin.

may have trouble finding it. Try a model airplane hobby shop, or a specialty lumberyard. For fish up to 5 pounds, soft pine can be used, but it is more difficult to work with.

Another option for medium-sized fish is a chunk of green Styrofoam, the kind used in floral arrangements. Keller says green Styrofoam is much superior to white foam plastic, and it can be shaped easily with a sharp knife.

With scissors, cut out the silhouette you drew on the heavy paper. Place this pattern on the block of balsa wood or Styrofoam and trace it. With a coping saw or jig saw, cut the body to this shape. Make the big end slightly longer than the pattern as this will extend into the fish's head slightly, to give support *(illustration 7-10)*. A wood rasp and knife are used to model the mannequin into the general shape of the body *(illustra-*

7-8. A tablespoon makes a good instrument for scraping the skin.

7-9. When you are finished, the skin should be completely free of flesh.

7-10. Using the paper pattern, a body is cut from wood or Styrofoam.

7-11. Using a wood rasp to model the mannequin.

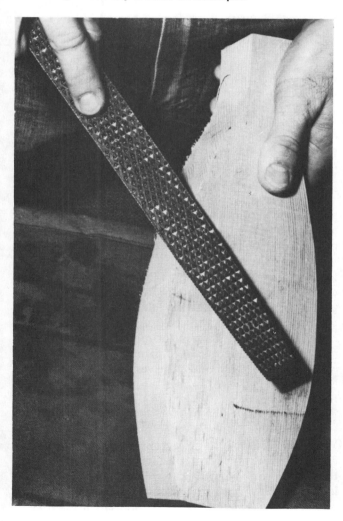

tion 7-11), following the fish's actual body as a guide. While the pattern supplies the length and width, the actual body helps in determining the true depth. The body mannequin does not have to be absolutely perfect, as you can use either clay or papier-mâché (see appendix) to fill in the places on the mannequin where the skin tends to sag. However, if the mannequin is too large, the fish will not appear in proper proportion.

To obtain a lifelike mount the mannequin should be slick and smooth and slightly smaller than the paper pattern. Use medium-grade sandpaper to smooth it.

According to Taxidermist Jimmy Bird, still another option is to prepare a body using excelsior and twine. With one exception, the fish form is made exactly the same way you make a bird mannequin. You'll also need a piece of board in the body for hanging the finished mount on the wall. Remove the body and use it as a guide while wrapping the excelsior. When the body is about 75 percent of its finished size, place the board on the side of the form that will lie against the wall, then secure the board with excelsior and add more layers until you have the right size. Use papier-mache to shape the mannequin and fill in those places where needed to achieve an exact fit.

And finally, you can make your own urethane forms as well. Follow the instructions in Chapter 13, *Sculpturing.* Once you have the mold, all that's needed is to drill an access hole in the plaster so you can pour the liquid right into the cavity. Experiment with smaller fish; for large fish, you're better off ordering a form from a taxidermy supply house.

Step 5 —*Mounting*

Remove the skin from the refrigerator and submerge it in water, to thaw it completely and get it thoroughly wet again. Rub the inside of the skin with borax, getting into every crease and corner. Borax preserves the skin, preventing decay, and kills odor.

Position the skin around the mannequin and draw the "show" side snugly into place. If any spots need filling out, add clay or papier-mâché. Then, anchor the skin to the mannequin, using one nail at the top and one at the bottom. This holds the skin firmly in place, making it easier to work with.

Mold a small amount of potter's clay or fire clay around the base of the tail to secure it to the mannequin.

7-12. Pull the skin together and anchor it to the mannequin with nails.

Also put some clay or papier-mâché at the base of each fin for anchoring. Clay or papier-mâché also goes around the end of the wood that extends into the head, to fill out places where flesh was removed and to secure the mannequin to the head. Once you finish the basic mounting and close up the fish, you can position the fins naturally by pushing them into their clay bases.

Pull the skin on around the mannequin and bring the two edges of the incision together, then nail along each side with No. 2 fine nails *(illustration 7-12),* spacing the nails about one-half inch apart. Be careful to keep the skin straight and avoid folds and bulges. Turn the fish over, finished side up, and cram more clay or papier-mâché deep into the mouth, to make the head stand up. Either position the fish's jaws open (avoid having them so wide as to appear unnatural), as in *(illustration 7-13)* or bring the jaws together naturally and wrap them with string to hold them in place until the mount dries, thereby creating a closed-mouth mount *(illustration 7-14).*

Cut some strips of light cardboard for the tail and fins. Place a piece of cardboard behind each fin and spread the fin naturally on it, anchoring it on each side with a straight pin pushed through the cardboard to hold it in this shape. Now place another strip of cardboard on top of the fin and secure the two pieces of cardboard together with bobby pins *(illustration 7-15).* Do this for all fins and the tail. Put the dorsal fin up naturally and drive a sharp piece of wire or a long nail into the top of the mannequin, at the place where the front spine of the fin can be hooked around it, holding the fin up and in natural position for drying. Sometimes it is necessary to prop up the fins and tail with blocks of wood to keep them in natural position until the clay or papier-mâché dries and secures them permanently. On an open-mouth mount, you also may have to prop the mouth with sticks of wood until the mount dries.

Now put the mount in a dry, shady spot and leave it for 2 or 3 weeks, depending on the weather, or until it is dry. The glass eye can be positioned any time prior to painting the mount. Place a small amount of clay in the eye socket and push the eye into place. On an open-mouth mount, the inside of the mouth also needs to be modeled before the mount is painted. Smooth enough clay around in the mouth to give it a natural look.

Step 6 —*Painting*

The last step is perhaps the most important of all. With animals and birds, the realism originates with the creature's eyes and ears, or the relationship between them and the body. With a fish the realistic appearance is derived chiefly from the coloration. A poor mount with a first-class paint job will be more realistic than a

7-13. A black bass mounted with its mouth open.

7-14. A closed-mouth mount of a black bass.

quality mount haphazardly painted.

Obtain three or four tiny paintbrushes with fine, soft bristles. It is better to have a brush for each color than to attempt to clean the brush each time you change paints. You can use either lacquer or oil paint, but do not mix the two. Stick with one or the other.

Apply a base coat of white paint, either with a brush or by using a pressurized can of white spray paint. The coat should be very, very light. This base coat also will serve as the white underside. Apply two or three very light coats rather than one moderately heavy one. Every scale should stand out individually when the base paint dries. If the paint is too thick, you won't be able to distinguish the scales and the fish will not have a lifelike appearance.

On the back, for best results apply a coat of dark green paint first; then add a light coat of black up high on the back, to give a dark-back effect. The lateral line is brushed down the center of the fish. If any other coloring, such as black dots or splotches which are found on

7-15. A mount with the mouth propped open and the fins and tail covered with cardboard.

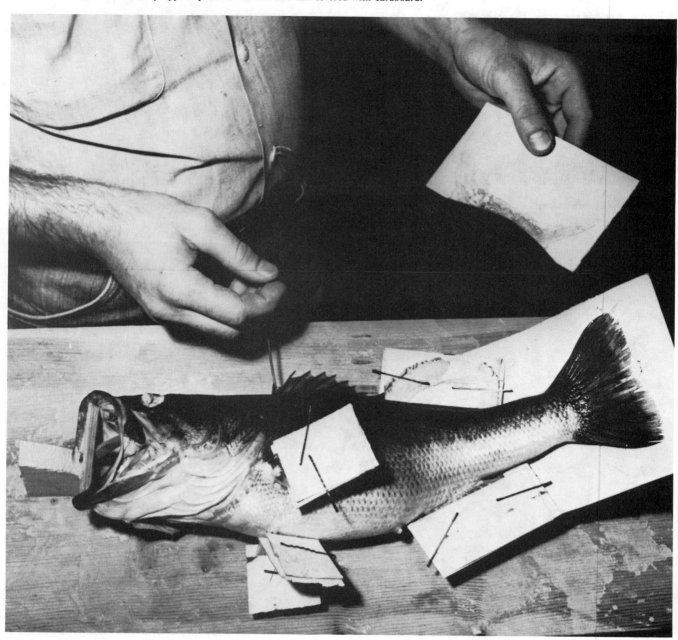

some bass, is needed, it can be added later, when the lateral line has dried. In painting a fish, use very little paint and lots of thinner. The paint should be almost like water. Many brushings will be needed to cover a spot, but the thin paint will allow the fish's natural markings to show through, making it appear that the coloration is actually in the scales, not over them. Keep the color photograph handy and follow it when selecting the colors and for the placement of individual colors. The inside of the mouth, if it is an open-mouth mount, should be painted a dirty white.

After all paint has completely dried, give the fish two or three very light coats of clear varnish, whether you painted with lacquer or oil paints. This gives the mount a shiny, wet, finished look.

Almost any plaque or shield can be used. Position the fish on the plaque where it looks most natural, then anchor it with a pair of 2-inch wood screws, running them through the back of the plaque, about 4 inches apart, into the mount. Add two screw eyes on the top of the plaque, roughly 6 to 8 inches apart, with which to hang the plaque. This finishes your mount; now all you need to do is find a suitable place to display your handicraft.

8/Large Fish

8/Large Fish

The term "large fish" could refer to any species that grows to extraordinary proportions, but here we are concerned with the popular billfishes: sailfish, marlin and sawfish.

Mounting any of these fishes is no simple undertaking and should never be attempted as a "starter job." For one thing, it is a complicated process, since the fish must be literally taken apart and reassembled. In a way it is a combination of two processes discussed earlier: making a mold to create a plastic fish (chapter 3) and the step-by-step procedure for mounting a black bass (chapter 7)—skinning, utilizing some sort of mannequin, and painting.

Besides being complex, the mounting of a large fish is expensive. The size alone demands an abundance of material, such as the plaster required to make a huge mold. The smaller the mount, the less materials needed, and thus the lower overall outlay. That is why we recommend smaller specimens for learning.

The Mold

The first step is to determine the fish's true dimensions. This is most easily done by making a drawing or crude blueprint. From this drawing you can later take the measurements you need. Choose a place where you have ample room to work. The very size of the fish demands quite a bit of space, which is another drawback if you are doing the job at home. Spread out a sheet of paper larger than the fish. Any paper which comes in rolls and is of adequate width will do. On the paper, position the fish the way you want it in the finished mount. Leave the sail (the big dorsal or top fin) folded down inside and draw around the fish, including the bill and tail. If you make any mistakes, do the job over.

Next, place the fish on a table larger than it is and start building up around it with sand, following the procedure for making a mold described in chapter 3 for a plastic fish. As in making the drawing, position the fish as you want it in the finished mount. The sail should still be folded down.

After you have poured the plaster on this side and it has dried completely, turn the fish over. Get somebody to help you do this. If possible, keep the fish from coming out of the mold but if it does you can replace it, being sure to put it back exactly as it was. This side will be slightly flatter, having been weighted down by the plaster. This is the way you want it, since this side will be against the wall on the finished mount and being flatter it will be easier to hang and the fish will have a more lifelike appearance.

Once the mold is completed *(illustration 8-1)*, you are

ready to start skinning, or "taking the fish apart."

Skinning

Step 1—Removing the Sail

Cut the sail off in the fold along the back, using tin snips or dykes (wire cutters). (You may need both, since the rays of the sail are extremely tough and difficult to cut through.)

Step 2 —Detaching the Tail

An ordinary meat saw will suffice. Cut through the body where the tail section begins to get larger.

Step 3 —Removing the Bill and Underjaw

Saw off the head just behind the gill covers. Don't worry about damaging the gill covers; these won't be used. They will be artificially reconstructed.

Step 4 —Preparing the "Show" Side

This is the side you molded first, the one which will be seen when the mount is completed. Before starting, you may want to remove the long pectoral fin just behind the gill cover; it might get in your way. You can take off the remaining fins later. Cut along the belly and back (most of the back already is cut from removing the sail). Instead of actually skinning the fish, remove the whole side as you would in filleting a fish—that is, cut through the flesh and leave it attached to the skin. In removing the side, it is easiest to start from the front, where you sawed off the head, and work back. Once you have the side free, lay it down, flesh up, and with a tablespoon scrape the flesh from the skin. With this method there is less likelihood of damaging the skin.

Step 5 —Removing the Fins

Take off the long fin behind the gill cover on the show side, if you haven't already done so; then remove the anus fin and the two small fins, one on top and one on bottom, near the tail. These small fins can easily be overlooked. The two long depth (hang down) fins on the forward part of the belly can be reconstructed from metal, but you should take their measurements for later reference.

You now have removed all the parts you need and the remainder of the carcass can be disposed of. But before doing so, be sure you have all the necessary parts: sail, tail, bill and lower jaw, skin from show side, and four fins *(illustration 8-2)*.

Preparing Parts for Mounting

Wash the sail, spread it on a piece of plywood, and tack it down. Tears can be repaired with a needle and No. 60 thread. All flesh must be removed from the base of the sail. The other fins can be tacked on the same plywood. Let the sail and fins dry indoors, away from the sun, which would damage them. You will not need the sail and fins until later; a replica will be made of the sail by casting.

The tail and head must be boiled in water to remove

LARGE FISH

TOOLS
Sharp knife
Kitchen knife
Tablespoon
Teaspoon
Hammer, small nails and tacks
Pliers
Tin snips or dykes (wire cutter)
Meat saw
Wood rasp

SUPPLIES
Sand
Piece of paper larger than fish
Pencil
10 pounds molding plaster
Red resin building paper
Yellow dextrin glue
Block of wood, cut from a two-by-four
Piece of plywood larger than sail on fish's back
No. 60 thread needle
1 quart molding rubber
1 gallon marine resin and catalyst (hardener)
Glass cloth, 7 square feet
6 strips 10-gauge metal, ½ inch wide and 8 inches long
Metal plate, 8 inches square
Burlap or cotton
1 pound box Bondo (automobile dent filler)
Papier-mâché
Glass eye
20 Mule Team Borax
Lead-free gasoline
Aerosol can of lacquer (color as desired)
Sandpaper

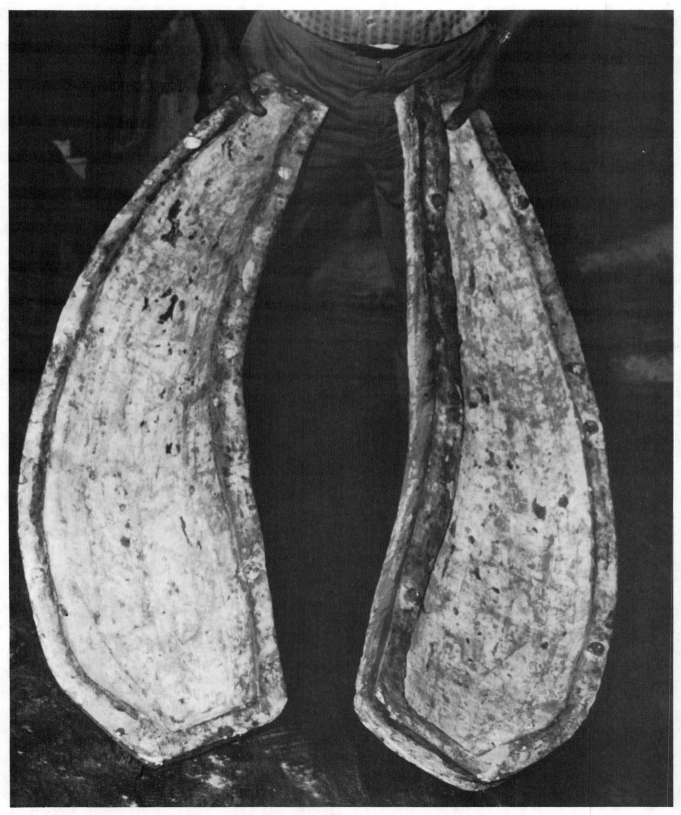

8-1. A finished mold, to be used for building a mannequin. Or order a urethane form from a taxidermy supply house.

PARTS OF FISH TO BE SAVED

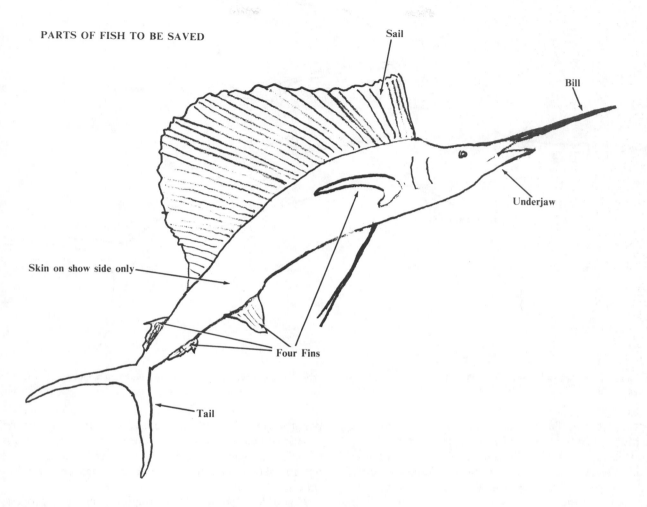

8-2. Before throwing any parts away, check to be sure you have everything you need.

8-3. Mannequin for a sailfish. (Disregard the strip of plywood along the back; it is difficult to attach to the mannequin and is really not necessary for support.)

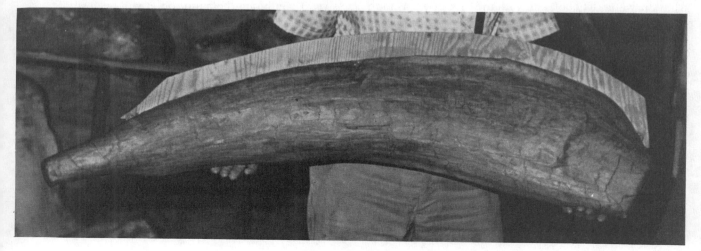

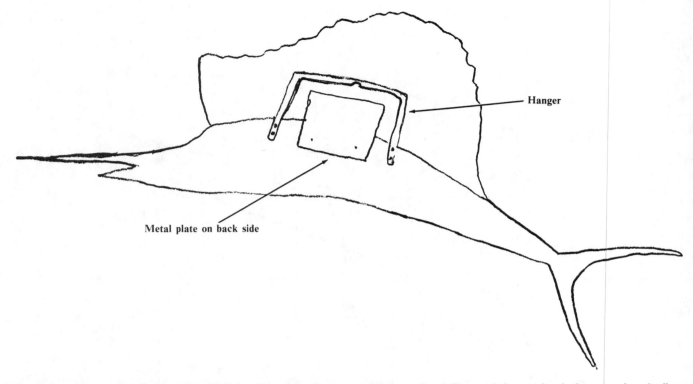

Hanger

Metal plate on back side

8-4. A hanger is attached to a block of wood built into the mannequin; use two screws at each end. The metal plate overlaps both mannequin and sail for added support.

flesh and fish oils. The container need not be as large as a washtub, since the fleshy part of the head is boiled, not the bill. Separate the tail flutes by sawing straight back. This allows the removal of all gristle and flesh. Boil only the part of the tail that was attached to the body, not the pointed ends of the flutes. While these are boiling, wrap the skin and put it in the refrigerator. Nothing needs to be put on it. You can store it in a plastic bag.

After about an hour of boiling, test the flesh with a fork. If it comes off easily, remove the head and tail from the water, let cool, and with the fork or a teaspoon scrape all the flesh away.

The tail, like the sail, should be tacked on a piece of plywood, otherwise it will warp and dry crooked. Hang the head and bill in a safe place. Both sections should be dried indoors, not in the sun.

While these parts are drying you can construct the mannequin *(illustration 8-3)*. Follow the instructions in chapter 12, using red resin building paper (20-pound weight), and yellow dextrin glue. One significant alteration is needed, however: Place a block of wood inside the half that will be against the wall when the finished mount is hung. A section of a 2-by-4 will do. This will provide a support for the bracket or hanger *(illustration 8-4)*.

Put the mannequin aside to dry, and while it is drying,

begin to get the other parts ready. Since there is a drying time involved with each step, the entire project will obviously take some time. But don't hurry. Let each part dry properly. As I have emphasized, taxidermy takes time and patience.

If you don't want to go through this creative process, you can order a urethane mannequin from a taxidermy supply (see Appendix). Specify the species and include measurements for the fish's total length and girth. Be aware, however, that mannequins for big fish are expensive; if you botch the paint job, it will be costly.

Making the Sail

By the time you have finished the mannequin, the sail should be dry. To make a cast of it, you will need a quart of molding rubber, available from Reel Trophy, a taxidermy supply house (see appendix).

Detach the sail from the plywood. It should be not only dry but clean. The nail holes or other blemishes can be patched with paper on the underside and a little mineral wax or beeswax on top.

Caution: Make sure you are working on the show side of the sail, the side from which you removed the skin. If you get it reversed, the result will be somewhat like try-

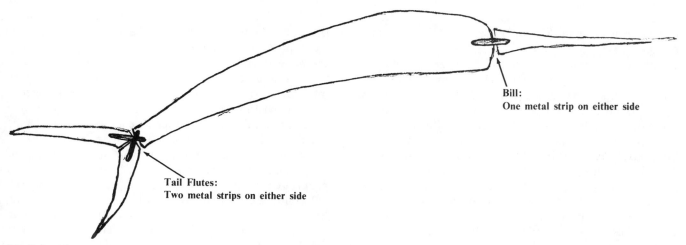

Bill:
One metal strip on either side

Tail Flutes:
Two metal strips on either side

8-5. Strips of metal are used on each side to attach the bill and both tail flutes.

ing to put a right shoe on your left foot. If necessary, hold the sail atop the mannequin to doublecheck that you are working with the correct side.

With the sail flat on a piece of plywood or glass, show side up, apply the molding rubber, using a kitchen knife to spread it on about one-eighth inch thick. If you can't attain this thickness the first time, spread the rubber evenly, allow to dry an hour or two, and then spread another coat.

Once you are satisfied with the job, allow the rubber coating to dry at least 24 hours, perhaps longer, depending on the humidity. To determine when it is ready to come off, simply lift some of the excess along the edges. If this peels off cleanly and the rubber is solid, the entire covering can gingerly be pulled off. Go slowly and avoid tearing. As extra insurance, lay the rubber sail on a flat surface and let it dry a few more hours. If handled properly, this rubber sail or "mold" can be used time and again. Consequently, if a professional taxidermist makes an artificial sail for, say, a 7-foot sailfish, and sometime later wants to mount another fish of comparable length, he can use the same rubber mold without the expense and bother of molding another one.

For making the actual stiff sail to put on the mount, you need a gallon of marine resin and several sheets of glass cloth, the same ingredients which go into manufacturing a fiberglass boat. You should be able to get these materials from a local boat dealer.

How many glass cloth sheets you need depends on the cloth's thickness. In most cases two or three sheets will suffice. Overall you want the sail to be roughly one-eighth inch thick. Along the base, however, an extra strip or two of glass cloth, about 1 inch wide, must be added to make the base flare to about one-quarter inch along the edge in order to provide extra strength and support.

Mix 1 quart of resin with hardener according to the directions on the can. These must be stirred together thoroughly to achieve optimum results.

Pour about half the mixture (or 1 pint), onto the rubber mold, then spread it evenly with a kitchen knife. Spread glass cloth over the resin and spread a little more resin over the cloth, afterward pressing it down all over to eliminate any trapped air bubbles. Using the same procedure, add another layer of cloth, or maybe two more, until you have the desired thickness. Then use extra strips to build up along the base.

Allow the glass cloth to harden or "set up" and then gently peel off the rubber. Complete hardening takes at least 10 hours and sometimes slightly longer, depending on the weather. Once you have separated the rubber mold, place the glass cloth sail on a flat surface and allow it to cure, which requires several days.

If you should damage the sail, it is a simple matter to take the rubber mold and start again. But remember that resin, hardener and glass cloth are expensive. For the same reason be gentle when peeling away the rubber mold; when you have bought a quart of molding rubber you will understand why.

Preparing The Mannequin

The sailfish will begin to take shape as you add the bill and tail to the mannequin, which must be thoroughly dry. The drying time will vary with the climate and weather; the more humidity the slower it dries.

To attach the bill and tail you will need six strips of 10-gauge metal about one-half inch wide and 8 inches long, or a comparable substitute. This metal can be obtained at any sheet metal shop.

You also need to mix about a teacupful of resin and hardener. About 1 gallon of resin is required for the entire mounting job, but mix only the amount you need for any given step.

Take two of the metal strips and, at the end of each, bend about one-half inch at a 90-degree angle. This bend serves as an anchor to secure the metal with resin. Place the bent end of one strip in the bone at the base of the bill on either side. These will secure the bill firmly to the mannequin *(illustration 8-5)*. Now glue the metal to the bone, using resin mixed with burlap. The resin-burlap mixture should be of thick enough consistency that it will not run. Burlap can be obtained by cutting a so-called tote sack (or tow sack) into very fine pieces. If you are unable to find burlap (most stock feeds now come in paper bags), cotton can be substituted. Just stir the prepared resin and the burlap or cotton together and pack the mixture around the bent end of the metal, in the skull or the base of the bill. When you get one strip positioned, add the other on the opposite side, then finish packing the cavity with resin, keeping it all inside the bone structure.

Use the same procedure on the tail section; a strip of metal on each side to hold the flutes in place *(illustration 8-5)*. When this step is completed, you will have metal strips protruding from either side of the bill and tail, which will later be attached to the mannequin.

Spread the paper drawing on a flat surface, place the mannequin on it, and position the head and tail at appropriate ends. By using the drawing as a guide you can determine the proper position of skull and tail. Part of the mannequin may have to be trimmed away at one or both ends to get the exact overall length of the original fish.

8-6. Taxidermist Lem Rathbone showing a sailfish he mounted.

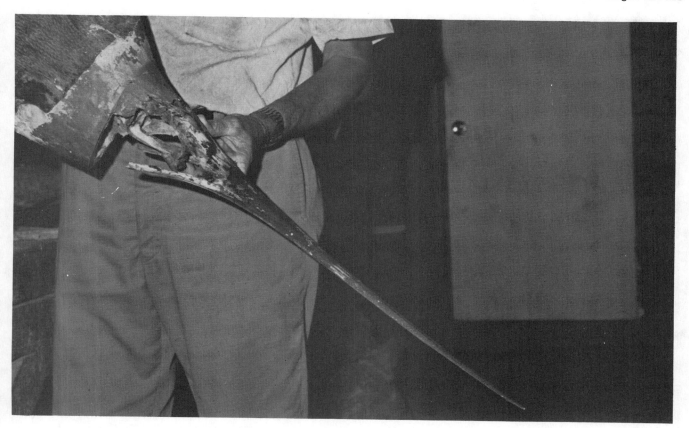

8-7. The cleaned bill goes right back into place.

8-8. The skin is put back on show side, overlapped onto the back, and attached with closely spaced nails. This rough edge will be covered with Bondo.

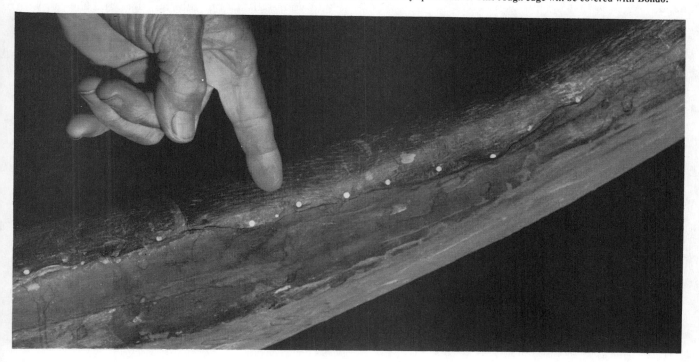

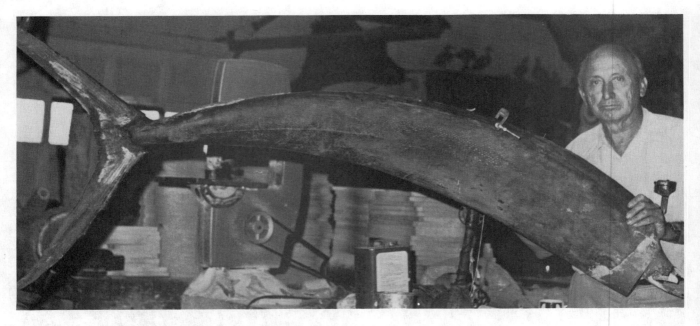

8-9. This is the way the mannequin looks with the skin back in place.

At this stage it is important to get everything in the precise shape you want it. Nail or screw the metal strips to the mannequin to hold the bill and tail in place while you fasten both securely with more resin mixed with burlap or cotton.

Place the skin on a flat surface, finished side down, and completely cover the part of it which goes onto the mannequin with borax, rubbing it all over with your hand.

Spread the skin over the mannequin and tack it into place, being sure to eliminate air pockets. If you have a flat place on the mannequin where the skin seems to sag, build it up with papier-mâché. If the skin doesn't completely reach to top and bottom, or there is a bit of overlap that goes onto the back, don't worry—you can correct this later.

Once the skin is in place, smooth it all over, using a wet cloth and dipping the cloth in water periodically. When everything appears all right, leave the mount alone for a week to 10 days, depending on the weather, or until it is completely dry.

To finish prior to painting, spread a thin layer of Bondo along the edges that were tacked. This will cover the tacks, any crinkles in the skin, and any rough edges. Also use Bondo (automobile dent filler, available at most auto parts outlets) to fill in the section between the tail flutes.

The dried fins can be used just as they are. Add the pectoral fin, just behind the head, on the show side only. Secure it with a tiny nail, then put some resin mixed with burlap or cotton (Bondo also can be used) around it for

a permanent anchor. Do the same thing with the top and bottom fins just forward of the tail and with the larger anus fin. Cut the two long depth fins from metal, using the measurements you took earlier. Drill two holes in mannequin to accept these fins and secure them permanently with resin or Bondo.

Once the resin and Bondo harden, you can smooth the edges with a rasp to get clean lines. Once everything is to your satisfaction, rub the edges and the tail with sandpaper for a smooth finish.

The addition of the sail is the last step before the painting. The sail will have rough edges that need cleaning up. Hold the sail atop the fish and mark the lower edge so you can cut it to match the contour of the back, something like cutting one board to fit another. You also will need to use a rasp and sandpaper to smooth the ragged top edge of the sail. On a resin and glass cloth replica there will be rough spots which must be eliminated. Smear a layer about one-quarter inch thick over the metal strips, overlapping quite a bit onto the mannequin to assure a firm hold. Don't worry if it isn't quite smooth since the strip on the show side will be covered later, and the one on the other side will be against the wall and hidden by the mount. Allow to dry about a day or until the resin is completely "set up."

Make a hanger of some sort, attach it to the block of wood in the mannequin and hang the mannequin on the wall. Now you can begin to see what you are going to have. Use resin mixed with burlap or cotton to glue the lower jaw. It slips right into place. You can secure it with wire until the resin hardens.

Next prepare some papier-mâché and model the head, building up and forming the gill covers (or coverlets). Here is where your imagination comes into play. Add papier-mâché until everything looks right, also filling out under the chin. Do not try to complete the job with one application. Stay slightly under the edge, about one-eighth inch; this you can finish with Bondo. This putty-like substance is easy to work with and provides a smooth surface that can be sanded and painted for a better finish.

Before using the Bondo, add the glass eye (specify type of fish when ordering from taxidermy supply house.) Build up the papier-mâché a little at the eye socket, position the eye, and then stand back and check its appearance. The reason for placing the eye at this time is that Bondo hardens quickly and you might find the eye permanently affixed before you get the correct angle. Later you can use Bondo to smooth around the eye.

Once you have the head shaped, cover the entire mannequin with a thin application of papier-mâché. This covers up or corrects any blemishes. After it dries, you can follow with another light coat of Bondo, at the same time that you add the Bondo to the head. Always keep in mind the general contour and shape of the body. Extra papier-mâché and Bondo will be needed to fill the cracks where the bill and tail were attached.

Adding Skin and Fins

Be sure the skin is completely clean on the underside, all flesh scraped away. Rinse it in lead-free gasoline in an open, well-ventilated spot and hang it briefly to drain.

You probably will have some trouble getting the sail to fit the back contour exactly, but you can use Bondo to fill in or cover your mistakes. Don't fail to take advantage of this substance; it can correct a lot of errors.

Any piece of stiff metal, about 8 inches square, can be used to support the sail *(illustration 8-4)*. The exact dimensions are not important as long as the metal plate is small enough to remain hidden behind the sail and the mannequin.

Put a couple of nails or screws through the metal into the mannequin, leaving about half the metal sticking up above the back. Put the sail in place and let it rest against the metal. Use resin mixed with burlap or cotton to go along the back side of the lower end, where the sail fits on the back, using enough to secure it firmly, and also use the mixture to cover the metal plate with plenty of overlap on the sail and mannequin. Once the resin

8-10. Once the bill and lower jaw are glued into place, this is the way they will look.

hardens, glue along the front or finished side of the sail's lower edge with Bondo, as if you were caulking around a bathtub. You could use resin here, too, but Bondo is strong and easier to finish with sandpaper.

Except for color, your fish is now complete. Give it a final once-over for any flaws that need correcting. Use Bondo, rasp, and sandpaper for final finishing.

Painting

Spraying gives much better quality than does a brush. Aerosol cans are fine. Lacquer, either plain or acrylic, is superior to paint with. If you are unable to get lacquer, however, and start with paint, you must continue with paint. Never mix paint and lacquer.

Pick a well-ventilated spot for spraying. When you are with highly combustible substances, such as lacquer or the gasoline used for cleaning the skin, always be super-careful.

Begin with a coat of primer, allow to dry, sand lightly, and add another. Two or three light applications are much better than one heavier coat. Avoid runs. The primer should go over the entire fish: body, bill, tail, sail and fins. Give it ample time to dry between applications; it is recommended to allow each coat to dry overnight before proceeding. Sand and wipe clean.

Over the primer put a coat of aluminum lacquer, again covering the whole fish. Once this dries, sand it lightly with very fine sandpaper. This keeps the paint from chipping or flaking.

From here on you are on your own. Obtain a color photograph or painting of a sailfish and paint your mount accordingly. Even a professional like Lem Rathbone uses a color photograph as a guide, never relying on memory.

The belly will need a light touch of pearl essence. This doesn't show with any prominence but makes the finished mount look better. The lines of spots on a sailfish's body are lighter than either the back or the sail. The sail also has some black spots on it. A light spray of gold lacquer mixed with clear, down the body, centered halfway between top and bottom, from eye to tail, helps the appearance. The sail, tail, fins and bill should be trimmed in black. When you are satisfied with your paint job, allow it to dry thoroughly, then go over it with several applications of clear lacquer (or paint, if that is what you are using). Again use several light coats to avoid runs. This finish can be put on according to taste, but the more coats, the more the fish glistens and shines and looks lifelike.

There, at long last, you are through. We hope the results are worth the time, effort and headaches involved.

More on Painting Fish

Painting your fish mount is going to give you problems. This is a skill you must learn on your own.

"There is no way to tell someone how to paint a fish," explained Lem Rathbone, "just as there is no way to tell an artist how to paint a picture."

Recognize the problems and do the best job you can.

For one thing, fish of the same species that come from different waters won't have the same coloration. A black bass from clear spring water won't look like its cousin that lives in turbid water. If you take a color photograph of the specimen you caught and you wish the mount to appear as realistic as possible, you must blend the colors by trial and error, maybe first testing the paint on a piece of cardboard before you paint the mount.

There is a certain "stock" bass of greenish tints which you probably have seen duplicated many times. But take two bass paintings by different artists, put them side by side and study them, and you will soon notice that while generally they look alike, there are subtle differences. Each artist has his own concept as to what a bass looks like.

The black bass is only one example. The same principle applies to all fish species. Of course some species are easier to paint than others. A freshwater drum with its general grayish-drab coloration would be less complex to re-create than would a many-colored rainbow trout.

A taxidermist friend of Rathbone once brought a sailfish mount to him to ask where he had gone wrong; the paint job didn't look just right.

The friend had been fooled by colors. His inexperience showed in a blackish back and black-rimmed fins. Rathbone took one of his own mounts into bright sunlight and showed his friend that the color was not black but instead a very dark blue.

This brings up another problem. It is difficult for the inexperienced painter to know precisely which shades of color to purchase. The difficulty is compounded by the fact that different manufacturers have different names for essentially the same colors in paints or lacquers. Consider the very dark blue lacquer used on a sailfish. One manufacturer calls his brand "marlin blue," while another labels his "India blue."

Rathbone gets his best results by mixing colors to achieve the shade he wants. But this requires experience.

So do not expect perfection at first. After you paint a mount, look at it critically and attempt to see what you did wrong. Continually strive to improve. Taxidermy is a never-ending learning process.

Another thing to keep in mind is that you are painting the mount, first, to please yourself and, second, to please others. If you are satisfied with the finished job, others undoubtedly will be also. But every person "sees" differently, so do not be surprised if some praise your work while others criticize it. But don't be swayed too much either way by what others say. Mount and paint the fish to please yourself.

Yet while the artistic part (the blending of shades and colors) can't be explained in a book such as this, the technical part can.

One more time it should be stressed that most fish-mount paint jobs are inferior not because of the choice of colors but rather because of the way the paint is applied. The most common mistake is to put the paint on too thick, which obscures everything underneath. Rathbone prefers lacquer since it can be applied very thin. It is as if the first couple of applications are not there at all. Continually adding superthin coats brings out the colors, yet the finish remains transparent, so that details, such as scales, show vividly. Final touches make a significant difference—a spot of red or black or whatever color is needed to bring out the highlights.

Again, don't forget that paint and lacquer will not mix. You must stay with whichever one you start with.

If your initial paint job is bad, trying to improve, or even repainting invariably makes it worse. Paint or lacquer remover is no solution either. It is almost impossible to get the mount clean enough to repaint without breaking something, usually the delicate fins or tail. Just write the job off to experience and attempt to do better with the next mount.

9/Fish Replication

9/Fish Replication

If you consider yourself a sportsman as well as a home taxidermist, you may well find your interests in conflict. Once you've caught a "wall hanger" fish, your emotions will tug in opposite directions. You'd like to release the fish, but you'd also like to mount it. Thanks to replication, you can now do both.

Webster defines replication as the "process of reproducing." In other words, you don't need the fish; all you need are the fish's measurements. These measurements are then used to duplicate the fish you let go—it's a painted, fiberglass look-alike with exactly the same dimensions to hang on your wall with pride.

"Replication is a heck of a deal," says taxidermist Chris Streetman, "especially right now with everyone concerned about our fish resources. This option of reproduction makes everyone even more aware of conservation."

Replication is not new, really. It has only become more visible as more replicas of different fish species became available from the supply houses. Taxidermists have used replicas for a long time because, in some circumstances, it was a matter of necessity. Consider the catfish. Streetman says about the only usable parts of a catfish are its mouth and teeth. The whiskers aren't usable, nor are the front and rear dorsal fins. "The skin of a catfish won't cure properly," says Streetman. "It tends to swivel up.

This is true of any fish without scales. If you worked at it you could remove the delicate skin, take a crack at curing it and using it. But it's not worth the hassle, not with replicas available."

A shark, with no bones, can't be mounted with con-

FISH REPLICATION (SHARK)

TOOLS
Tin snips
Sandpaper, or moto tool
Strips of thin cardboard
Knife
Saber saw, or moto tool
Spray gun, brushes

SUPPLIES
Shark replica (to be ordered)
Glass eyes (to be ordered)
Bondo
Laquer

ventional taxidermy methods either. And with body cartilage only, it's almost impossible to skin. Most saltwater fish that are caught offshore—those with small scales or no scale structure—present another problem. "Their skins are so oily," says Streetman, "that it's very difficult to cure them out. Excess oil will ruin a paint job in no time flat. That's why professional taxidermists use repros."

While a home taxidermist can take his time and experiment, the professional taxidermist can't afford such luxury. Partly for that reason, replicas are advertised as an alternative to old taxidermy methods. "I can get a replica of about any species of fish you can think of," Streetman adds, "and probably some you've never thought of. A lot of taxidermy supply houses are making them now." Streetman, who is in his 20s, views his generation as more receptive to replication. Conservation has, after all, become a very important word in the vocabulary of young people in the 1990s.

All that's needed to mount a replica of a fish you've caught are its measurements, both length and girth. It

9-1. A sailfish replica.

9-2. A shark replica with fins in place.

also helps if you take a color photo of the fish immediately after it has been caught; or you can duplicate a full-color illustration of that same fish from one of several good fish identification guides. Some saltwater fish fade rapidly in color once they are taken from the water. Using the measurements and the photo (or illustration) as a color guide, it's possible to make a fish that looks exactly like the one you caught. No one can tell the difference between it and the real thing. There are also convenience and costs to consider. "Suppose you go out of the country and you catch a sailfish you want to mount at home," Streetman points out. "All you need are the measurements and then you can release it. You don't have to worry about carrying or shipping the fish home. Your replica will look just like a sailfish I'd mount in my own shop, assuming you have the expertise to paint the replica."

There are two ways to go with replicas. A complete replica is simply a look-alike of a certain fish, such as a sailfish *(illustration 9-1),* except for the glass eye. Or you can use a replica in conjunction with a few parts taken from a real fish, such as the gills of a largemouth bass, or the bill, tail and fins from a sailfish. The small blacktip shark replica illustrated in this chapter will, when completed, contain the teeth taken from the shark that was caught, but everything else is manmade replication.

A shark replica has all the fins in place *(illustration 9-2).* With many replicas, such as a bluegill *(illustration 9-3),* the fins are kept separate and must be cut out and attached to their appropriate places. This is not difficult, because slots on the replica indicate exactly where the

fins should be attached.

Fiberglass replicas filled with urethane foam require some preparation before painting. You can trim such a replica to shape with a pair of tin snips *(illustration 9-4).*

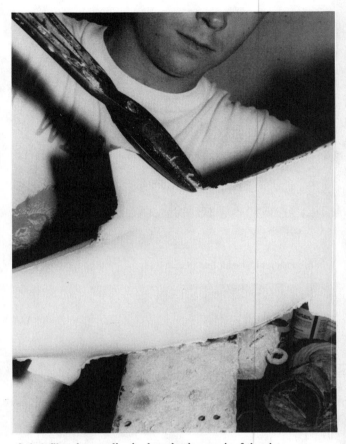

9-4. A fiberglass replica is shaped using a pair of tinsnips.

9-5. The top seam must be sanded down slightly below level.

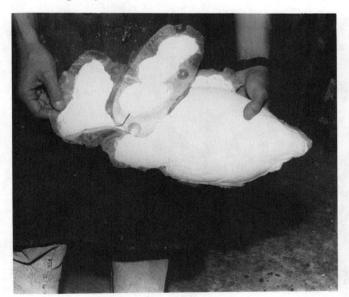

9-3. A bluegill replica.

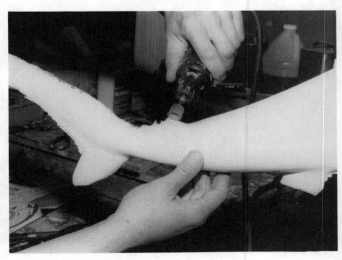

Fiberglass is tough, though, so you'll need some heavy-duty cutters. Once that job is done, smooth the edges with sandpaper.

Along the top of the replica, you'll note a raw seam line caused by the molding process. This seam must be eliminated. Even after sanding it smooth, the line will show once the fish has been painted. Streetman recommends sanding the seam down slightly below level *(illustration 9-5)*, creating a slight dip. Fill the dip with bondo, using a piece of thin cardboard as a spatula to apply a thin, smooth coat *(illustration 9-6)*. After the bondo hardens, it can be sanded, eliminating the seam line.

Next, the mouth must be cut to make room for the teeth *(illustration 9-7)*. Streetman uses a Dremel moto tool that most taxidermists prefer for drilling, cutting or sanding. You can also open the mouth with a saw—but proceed slowly and carefully. Once this chunk of fiberglass has been removed, the teeth can be positioned into place *(illustration 9-8)* and glued with bondo. The dried teeth are very fragile and break easily, so be careful. Once the teeth are in place, model the inside of the mouth with bondo, finishing with sandpaper after the bondo hardens.

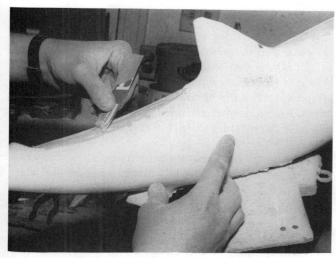

9-6. A thin, smooth coat of bondo is used to fill in the dip (see illus. 9-5).

9-7. The mouth of this replica is cut to make room for the teeth.

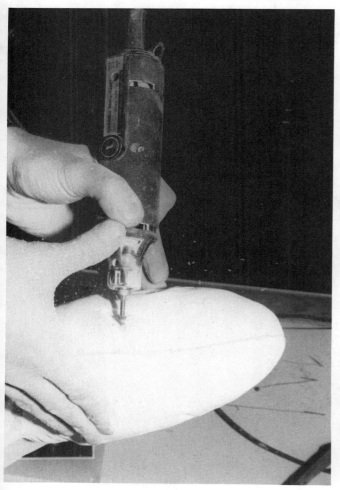

9-8. The teeth are set in place and glued with bondo.

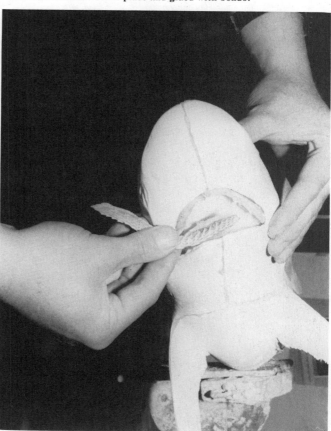

If you are mounting a black bass, for example, and you want the gill covers to be flared, here's what to do: follow the lines of the gill cover impression on the replica with a marking pencil. This bold outline will provide a good pattern to follow. Draw the line just outside the gill cover, about one line out. That way you won't cut off part of the gill cover. Use a circular saw or moto tool to cut completely through the fiberglass. Allow some extra cutting room around top and bottom. If you cut too far, the mistake can easily be filled with bondo. Cut the jaw down almost to the mouth.

Next, place the head of the replica under a heat lamp. Any light that radiates heat will do, but a heat lamp works best. Allow the gill cover to get hot all over. Then, with a large screwdriver inserted under the cut portion, apply slow, steady pressure to lift the gill cover. Once the cover is lifted, push wood wedges under it until the desired height is attained. Remove the replica from the heat and let it cool; now when the wedges are removed, the cover will remain open. Use sandpaper to smooth the edges and the inside of the opening (a moto tool or a round rasp can also be used). After the gills from the fish are dried and painted red, they can be glued in place. Use bondo to model inside the cavity resulting from the raised gill cover. After the bondo hardens, smooth with sandpaper. An alternative is to cut artificial gills from red felt, available at any cloth store (but real gills are much more lifelike).

The amount of preparation involved in this process really depends on the replica. Different styles are available from different supply houses. Take your time, study each step carefully, and you should encounter no problems.

Finally, paint using the same technique outlined in Chapter 7. This is a crucial step; be sure you have all the correct materials and plenty of time. Don't rush. If the replica isn't painted right, it won't look right, no matter how much effort and time you have put into the preparation.

10/Novelties

10/Novelties

Most beginning taxidermists think of a big-game animal in terms of a head mount and nothing else. Yet there are parts of a large animal—a deer, for example—which can be utilized in other ways by the home taxidermist. The hide might be tanned and made into an attractive rug (see chapter 11). The feet can be used for many purposes. A gun rack, the rifle resting on two up-turned feet, is the most elementary (illustration 10-1). But antlers can be mounted on a plaque with a gun rack underneath (illustration 10-2), or a lamp made from the feet (illustration 10-3), or an ash tray from one foot of an elk or moose (illustration 10-4).

One do-it-yourself taxidermist improvised an unusual coffee table from parts of a deer. The four feet he used for the table legs, and the top he covered with the tanned hide. That table is quite a conversation piece.

If you look at a taxidermy supply catalog, you'll be amazed at the number of forms available for designing novelties. For a basic novelty, such as the gun rack described in this chapter, the form can be homemade, but for more elaborate novelties, like the lamp stand, it is necessary to order a commercial form. Most home taxidermists do not have the ability or the specialized tools for making such pieces.

For the gun rack, however, everything you need can probably be obtained in your home town. A form for each foot is fairly simple to construct, but if you prefer you can order a ready-made form from a taxidermy supply house. You also can make your own shield or order one. No special shape is required on the shield; just make it oblong from any type of board and long enough so that the feet can be positioned about 20 inches apart. Sand it smooth and varnish it to the desired luster. Perhaps you'll have to glue several boards together to get one large enough for the shield. Use a good-quality glue. Ordinary pine is all right and least expensive (illustration 10-5).

The feet of whitetail deer, mule deer, antelope, wild sheep or animals of similar size are suitable for a gun rack. The forefeet will provide a better-looking finished job.

1 —Skinning

This step is the most difficult. Skinning a foot, while it appears simple, requires a good bit of time. Some of the cutting will be "blind" and probably you'll have to make several attempts before accomplishing your objective.

Let's assume you are using a whitetail deer. Remove the two front feet at the knee joints. Along the rear of the leg make a cut full length, to the hoof, or as far as you can go (illustration 10-6). Skin from the top, peeling

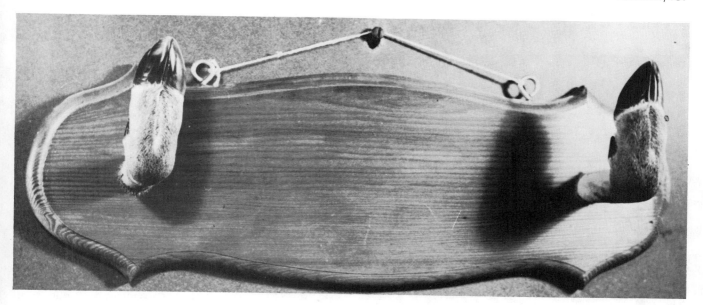

10-1. A gun rack made from a shield and two upturned deer feet.

the hide back until you pass the dew claw bone. Sever this bone *(illustration 10-7)*, leaving as little bone as possible with the claw. On each foot there are two claws, one on either side.

Now keep skinning down to the hoof. When you have advanced as far as you can go, it will be necessary to stick your knife blade down into the hoof and cut around the bone. Have a sharp knife blade and cut inward, toward the bone *(illustration 10-8)*. Nicks in the hide are almost impossible to repair. Attempt to twist the hoof free. If it

10-2. Mounted deer antlers, with the deer's feet as a gun rack.

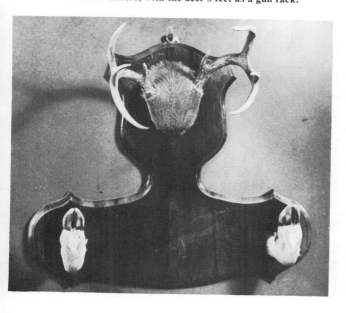

NOVELTIES
(Gun Rack from Deer Feet)

TOOLS
Sharp knife
Screwdriver
Coping saw
Drill with 5/16-inch bit and 1-inch wood bit
Wood rasp
1-gallon container

SUPPLIES
Glover's needle
Nylon fishing line, 6½-pound test
2 flat-head ¼-inch bolts 5 inches in length, with nuts
3¼ pounds salt
¼ pound alum
¼ pound 20 Mule Team Borax
2 boards, 1 inch thick, 4 inches wide, 5 inches long
Plaque
Polishing compound (to be ordered)
No. 220 sandpaper
Potter's clay or fire clay
2 screw eyes
String

10-3. A lamp stand improvised from three feet of a deer.

won't come loose, continue cutting around with your knife; you may have to go around the bone several times before you can sever all the tendons. Unless these wire-strong tendons are cut, it is impossible to twist the hoof free of the leg bone *(illustration 10-9)*.

When you have skinned both legs, broken both hoofs free, and completely separated the bone from the skin *(illustration 10-10)*, rub salt all over the fleshy side of the hide thoroughly. Stuff some salt into the hoofs to prevent spoilage. Place the hides in a dry, cool place and allow the salt to remove all moisture, a process that takes about 2 or 3 days.

Step 2 —*Pickling*

Put 1 gallon of water into a container and bring to a full boil. Add 2¼ pounds salt, one-quarter pound alum and one-quarter pound borax. Continue boiling until all the powders are dissolved. Then remove the liquid from the fire and permit it to cool completely.

Place the hides in the pickling solution and agitate them thoroughly. Leave them in the solution for about a week, agitating them every day or so.

Step 3 —*Preparing the Forms*

While the hides are pickling you can prepare the two forms for the gun rack *(illustration 10-11)*. Obtain a piece of lumber 1 inch thick, 4 inches in depth and at least 5 inches long. Finished lumber is seven-eighths inch thick, not a true inch; you'll probably have to obtain rough lumber from a lumberyard to get a piece thick enough to fill the feet adequately.

Cut the form to the pattern illustrated, making it 2½ inches high and 4½ inches long. Drill a 5/16-inch hold the full length of the form. Run a bolt through the hole, and countersink the head of the bolt where it won't show in the finished mount *(illustration 10-12)*.

With animals other than deer, before you skin the foreleg, bend it to the desired shape, lay it on a piece of heavy paper and trace around it to obtain a pattern which you will follow when making the form.

Use a wood rasp to round the edges, making the form more or less egg-shaped, in the approximate shape of a deer's leg. Check occasionally to see if the hide will fit around the form; take one of the hides from the pickle for fitting and then put it back. The tendency is to make the form too large.

Step 4 —*Mounting*

Remove the hides from the pickle, wash them in cool water with powdered detergent, rinse with cool water and allow them to drain. Stuff some clay into the hoof

10-4. This ashtray was made from a buffalo's foot, but a cow's foot could be substituted, or that of an elk or moose.

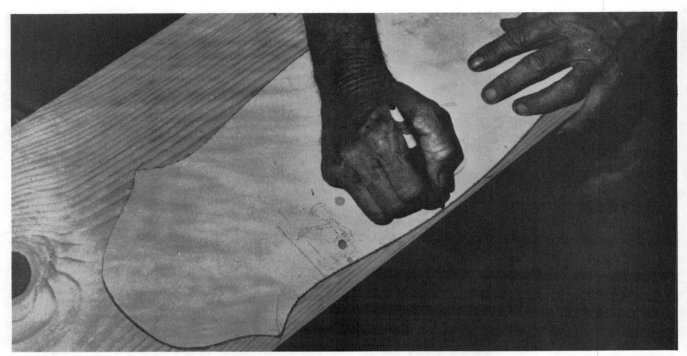

10-5. To make a shield, cut a pattern from cardboard, getting the exact shape and dimensions. Then brace the pattern onto a suitable board, cut it out with a band saw or coping saw, finish the board with sandpaper and varnish, and you are ready to add the two upturned deer feet to make a gun rack.

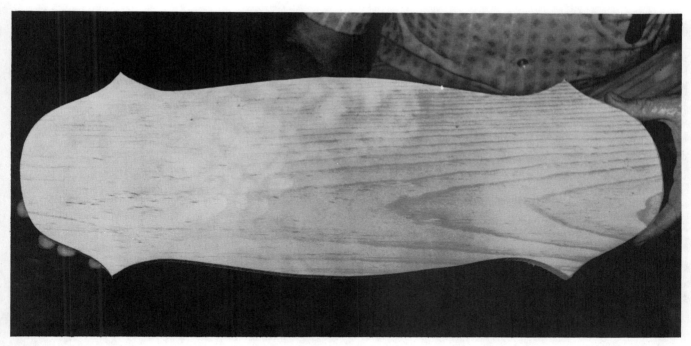

10-6. The finished product.

sections (two on each foot) to fill them out. Put clay around the countersink for the bolt head, rounding off the bend in the form to make it level with the wood. Position the core form inside the skin and sew it up, starting at the hoof and working to the end of the form. Leave the excess hide dangling until the mount dries; this allows for shrinkage. Pull the hoof sections of each foot together and tie them with string, so that they won't spread as the mount dries. Put the feet in a cool, dry spot and allow them to dry for at least 2 weeks. Drying inside the hoofs is a slow process.

Step 5 —*Finishing*

Sandpaper the hoofs until they are completely smooth. Then, using either a buffer or a polishing compound, available from taxidermy supply houses, on a rag, polish the hoofs to a high gloss. Polishing brings out the color. Vigorously rub the hoofs to the desired luster.

Trim off the excess hide at the back of the forms. Mount the two hoofs about 20 inches apart on the shield, a spread wide enough to hold a rifle. Countersink the nuts to allow the shield to lie flat against the wall. The way to accomplish this is to bore a pair of 5/16-inch holes for the bolts. Then from the back, using a 1-inch wood bit, go into the same holes about one-quarter inch. Avoid going too deep or you may ruin the shield. The nuts go into the countersinks *(illustration 10-13).* Add two screw eyes for hanging, placing one eye directly above each hoof. This completes the gun rack.

10-7. An incision is made the full length of the foreleg.

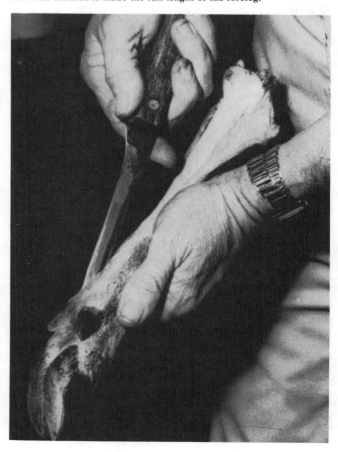

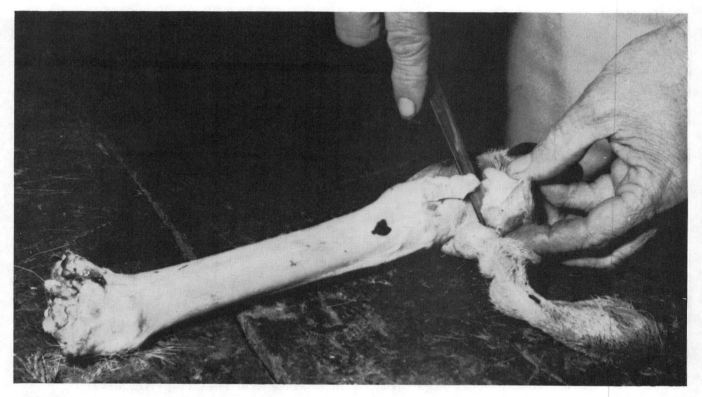

10-8. The dew claw bone is cut as close to the claw as possible.

10-9. You must push your knife blade into the hoof to cut the tendons.

10-10. Once the tendons are cut, you can break the hoof from the bone.

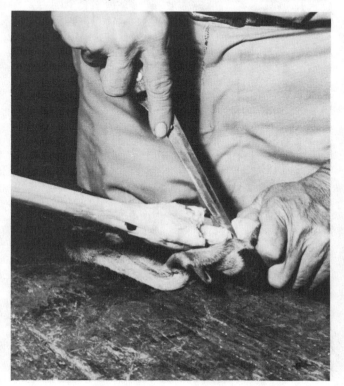

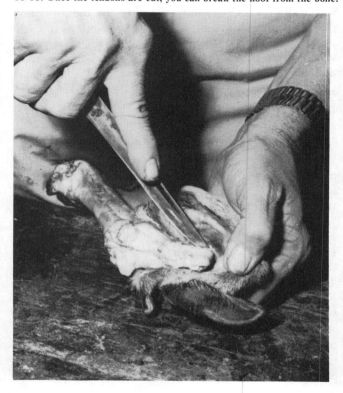

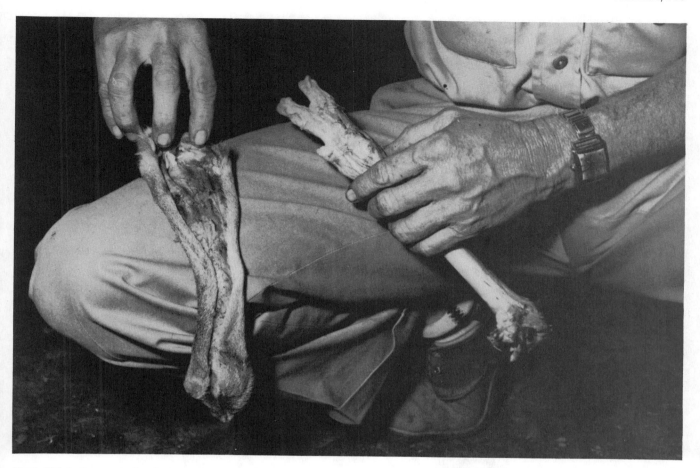

10-11. This is the way the foot looks when it is completely skinned.

10-12. The wooden form, right, is used to make the upturned foot, left.

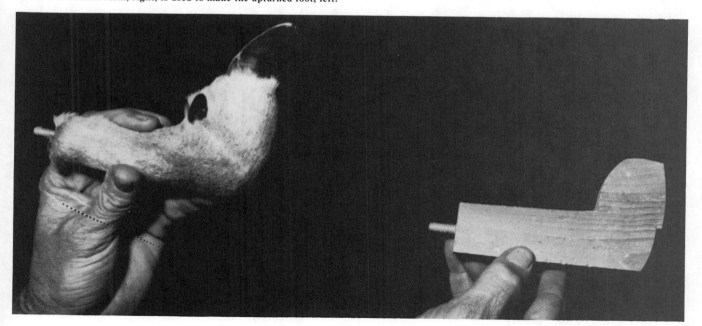

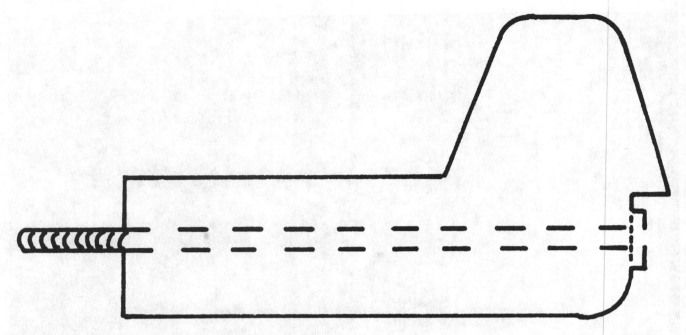

10-13. A bolt is run the length of the form with the bolt head countersunk.

10-14. The nut should be countersunk in the shield.

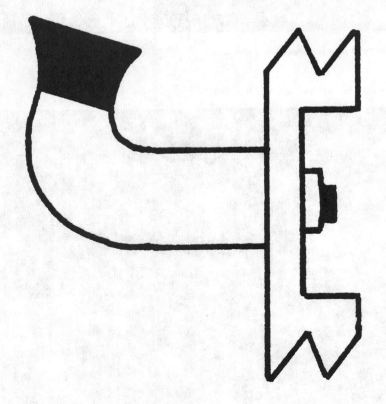

10-15. This unusual novelty was made by putting the so-called fan, or tail feathers, of a wild turkey gobbler on a shield. The rounded centerpiece with chopped-off bottom was improvised from a piece of buckskin.

11/Rugs

11/Rugs

Attractive rugs can be fashioned from hides of various wild animals. The hide of any of the wild cats—bobcat, cougar, ocelot, lion, and so on—makes a striking and durable rug, as does that of the bear and the coyote. Hides of antelope, elk and deer make poor-quality rugs since the hair tends to break. This chapter describes a rug made from a bobcat hide, but the basic plan is similar for any animal.

A rug made of the hide of a smaller animal, such as raccoon, can be hung on the wall. Even a rug from the hide of a large animal—bear, for example—can be hung for display purposes. The hide can be laid out completely flat or the head of the animal can be mounted on a mannequin. Instructions for making both types are given in this chapter.

We begin with the plain rug, with the entire hide, head and all, laid out flat.

Flat Rug

Step 1 —*Skinning*

Make an incision along the stomach of the animal, from just under the chin all the way to the base of the tail. Also cut down the inside of each leg, full length. Peel the hide both ways and skin to the tail. Peel out the

tail and split it on the underside, where salt can later be applied. Skin down the four legs. On a clawed animal, such as a bobcat or bear, the claws can be left on the hide; with hoofed animals, such as deer, cut the skin at the knee joint. Skin each leg just as you did with the squirrel (chapter 6), down each toe to the claws, skinning as far as you can go, then clipping the bone holding the claw, so that the entire foot remains on the hide.

Skin the head as you did with the squirrel, reversing the skin over the head and making no more incisions. Pay attention to the ears, eyes, mouth and nose. Turn the ears as you did with the big-game head mount (chapter 5). Once the hide is off, trim away any chunks of flesh and salt the hide thoroughly, in the tail, around the nose, along the edges, everywhere. Place it in a cool, dry place to drain for a couple of days. Then take it to a local taxidermist and ask him to send it off for tanning; tanneries usually do not accept hides from individuals.

Should you want to tan the hide yourself, refer to the tanning processes in chapter 14. But let me warn you that tanning is an arduous, time-consuming process.

Step 2 —*Ordering Supplies*

While the hide is at the tannery (tanning requires several months) you can order the necessary felt for

RUGS
(Bobcat)

TOOLS
Sharp knife
Tape measure
Hammer
Brush
Scissors

SUPPLIES
Salt
1 square yard felt (to be ordered)
2 square yards gabardine cloth
1 pound No. 2 fine nails
Glover's needle
No. 8 linen thread, same color as felt
Straight pins

making the border. Felt can be obtained from the supply sources listed in the appendix and comes in a wide variety of colors. About 4 yards of felt should suffice for the bobcat (felt comes in even yard lots—2, 4, 6 yards, and so on).

With larger or smaller animals, lay the hide out flat and with a tape measure get a rough estimate of its circumference. Order more felt than you think you'll need; the hide will be stretched later.

Gabardine, which is used to line the back side of the rug, can be bought after the hide returns from the tannery. It is available at most dry-goods stores.

Step 3 —*Stretching*

When the tanned hide is returned to you, submerge it in a container of water (a bathtub will do) and leave it for 6 to 8 hours. Do not let it remain in the water much longer, as prolonged soaking will cause the hair to slip.

While the hide is soaking, find a spot where you can tack it, a place that nails won't ruin. Perhaps you can put it on a barn door, on a wooden attic floor, or on a

11-1. A rug made from the skin of a bear.

discarded door or a piece of plywood.

Remove the hide from the container, drain away the excess water, and place the skin, hair side up, on the spot where you plan to tack it for stretching and drying. Drive a straight row of No. 2 fine nails down the center of the hide, from the tail to the head, spacing the nails 2 to 3 inches apart. Drive the nails in only about halfway, as they are to be removed later.

Now take one side of the skin and stretch it, spreading the legs out naturally. Put a nail in each leg to hold it, then go around the skin and anchor it securely, spacing the nails 2 inches apart. Stretch the opposite side the same way and also anchor it with nails. The legs should spread out at about the same angle on both sides; the idea is to make the rug symmetrical. The shape you get now will indicate how the finished rug will appear.

Brush the hide thoroughly, getting the hair to lie naturally, and allow it to dry for a week to 10 days. After the skin is completely dry, remove the nails, turn the hide over, hair side down, and with a sharp knife trim away the ragged edges of hide. Don't use scissors as this will cut the hair. Trim about the same amount of hide from both sides of the skin to retain the symmetry.

11-2. A rug-head assembly for a mountain lion.

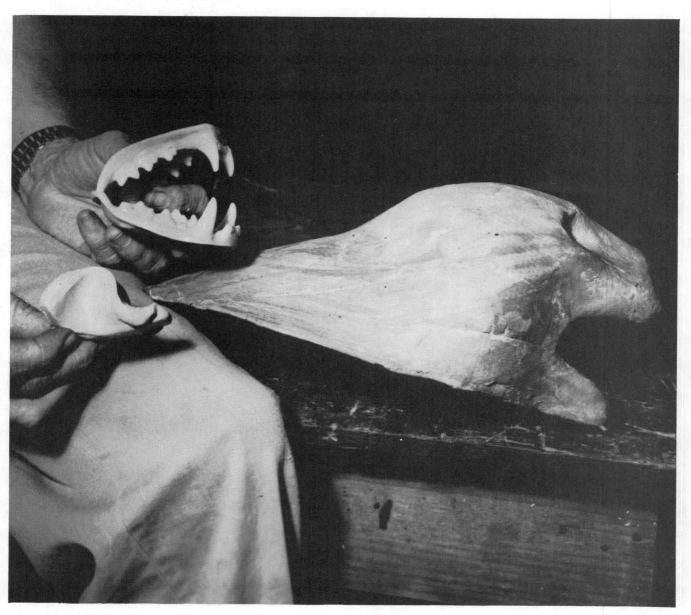

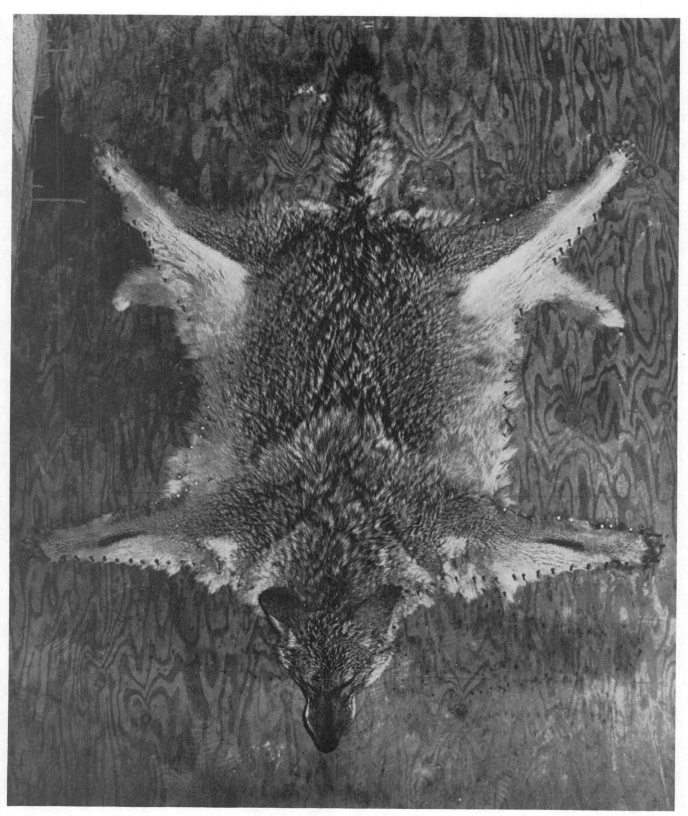

11-3. A coyote hide stretched to the proper shape and nailed to a sheet of plywood for drying.

11-4. Place the hide on the sheet of plywood to be used as a backing support and trace around it to make a pattern you can follow with a saw.

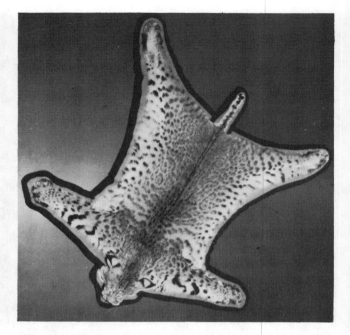

11-5. A rug can be made from a bear skin or from the skin from any other wild animal of appropriate size.

Step 4 —*Sewing*

Lay the rug flat, hair down, and position the felt border. The felt should encircle the hide completely, around the head and tail, and extend from the perimeter about an inch uniformly. Attach the felt border to the hide, using a glover's needle and No. 8 linen thread the same color as the felt, with a whip-stitch, about one-half inch between stitches. If you encounter difficulty with the corners, you may have to consult someone familiar with sewing techniques.

Once the border is attached all the way around, measure the length and width of the hide, at the longest and widest parts, and obtain gabardine enough to line the skin. Lay the gabardine flat and position the outstretched hide on it, hair up. Attach the felt border temporarily to the gabardine with straight pins, using enough to hold it securely. With a pair of scissors, trim the gabardine at the edge of the felt border, being careful not to cut the felt. Now turn the rug over, gabardine up, remove the pins, and tuck the ragged edges of the cloth under, to the edge of the skin. Using the same colored thread and whip-stitching, attach the gabardine to the hide, along the stitching you used to sew the felt border in place. This completes the rug.

Rug with Mounted Head

For a rug with a mounted head, you will need, in ad-

dition to the supplies listed for the basic rug, a rug-head assembly and glass eyes (see appendix for size; order from a taxidermy supply house), some potter's clay or fire clay, about a dozen No. 3 finishing nails, a small amount of plaster of Paris, beeswax, a small paintbrush and some black lacquer.

For an open-mouth mount, a rug-head assembly requires a mannequin and the animal's teeth and tongue. Place the teeth (the upper and lower dentures are attached) in the mouth of the mannequin and trim the edges of the gums and the mannequin with a knife until the teeth fit naturally. Then remove the teeth and position the tongue in the mouth properly and make two small holes with your knife blade about one-half inch apart through the back of the tongue and the bottom of the mannequin, matching the holes in the tongue with those in the mannequin. Run short pieces of wire through these holes and twist the ends together on the bottom side of the mannequin to hold the tongue firmly in place.

Now put the teeth back in the mouth. Mix some plaster of Paris, turn the mannequin upside down and work through the large hole in the bottom or flat side. Stuff plaster of Paris above and below the teeth to anchor them in place. Allow the plaster to dry.

After the hide has soaked and is draining, place some clay in the eye sockets and a small amount around the eyes and nose to hold the mannequin and the hide

11-6. Completed head mount of a bear, using a rug-head assembly.

together, and some more where the bases of the ears will be. Put the eyes in place.

Cut some liners from light cardboard and fill the ears to get them to stand up naturally. For a larger animal, such as a bear, you'll have to order appropriate ear liners.

Slip the mannequin into the head of the hide. Pull the nose into place and place a No. 3 finishing nail at the corner of each nostril to hold the nose properly. Position the lips on the open mouth and attach them to the mannequin with No. 2 fine nails, driven completely in and spaced about one-half inch apart. Position the eye sockets around the eyes and put a No. 3 finishing nail in front of and behind each eye. Anchor the ears in place.

To get a snarling expression, push the bottom and top of the nose together, to create wrinkles. Two No. 3 finishing nails must be used to hold each wrinkle in place, one at either end of the wrinkle. If you want three wrinkles, you'll need six nails, driven all the way in. These prevent the nose from stretching smooth again as the mount dries.

Now, as with the basic rug, spread, stretch and nail the hide; allow it to dry; trim it; and add the felt border and gabardine. In finishing, you'll also need to cover the nail heads around the lips and on the nose and fill in around the teeth with beeswax, filling the creases between the gums and the mannequin. Use a small paintbrush to add black lacquer on the nose and around the nostrils and eyes.

Wall Display

Skins of larger animals, such as bear, can be hung on a wall, but the hide tends to sag and get out of shape for lack of support. This is one reason that small animal hides are often used as wall hangings while larger hides are made into rugs.

If you would prefer to display a large skin on a wall, however, there is an alternate method. The steps—skinning, ordering supplies, and stretching—are exactly the same as those outlined for making it into a rug, either with or without the mounted head. The only difference is that for the felt backing you substitute something rigid, such as one-quarter-inch-thick plywood or a sheet of wall paneling. After the hide has been stretched and dried, remove it from the drying board and place it on the sheet of plywood. On some large animals you may need to do some gluing to get enough backing or to add leg extensions.

Take a pencil and trace around the hide *(see illustration 11-4).* Once you have a pattern, use a coping saw to cut the backing the shape of the hide, making it a fraction of an inch smaller all around so that the edge of the hide will overhang slightly to hide the backing.

Use an ordinary stapling gun to attach the hide to the board, spacing the staples about 3 to 4 inches apart. Spread the hair where you put a staple so that the hair will come back together and cover the staple. Short, small-headed tacks can be substituted for staples.

To hold the heavier head, drive three or four No. 3 finishing nails through the plywood from the back, into the bottom of the head mount. Hang the supported hide on the wall as you would hang a large painting.

12/Tricks with Antlers and Horns

12/Tricks with Antlers and Horns

While this chapter does not involve taxidermy in the strict sense, the amateur taxidermist may like to know about items that can be improvised from antlers and horns. There are many possibilities; your own imagination will probably present new ones. A table made from the horns of a longhorn steer, and lamps constructed from various bits of horn are among examples that I have seen.

Any of the projects outlined here will give you a "feel" of the subject. Once you master the fundamentals you can build all sorts of unique things.

Take a deer antler and with a saw remove all the points. With a ruler mark one-half-inch rings along the beam *(illustration 12-1)*. Saw along these lines and you'll have many circular disks. A hole can be drilled in the center of each piece. Sandpaper the bone and polish as desired. The disks can be used to make key chains *(illustration 12-2)*, earrings or a necklace *(illustration 12-3)*. You may want to varnish the disks for more luster.

A handsome and durable knife handle can be fashioned from the main beam of a deer antler. The type of knife will dictate the type of handle. A basic knife assembly, without the handle, is difficult to find; probably you'll have to buy a knife and remove its handle. One type of knife has a long, slender piece of metal that goes into the handle; another has a flat band, as wide as the blade, that goes between two halves of plastic, or whatever the handle is made of.

If the assembly has the long, thin piece of metal, obtain an antler with a fairly heavy beam and cut a section near the base *(illustration 12-4)* the desired length of the handle. Place this section in a vise and, with a drill bit approximately the same size as the piece of metal that goes into the handle, bore a hole horizontally into the bone, as near the middle as possible. The hole should not be the entire length of the handle, but only long enough to accept the long piece of metal that is attached to the blade. Probably you'll have to take out the bit and insert the piece of metal two or three times to measure the depth before you get it correct.

Mix some resin and catalyst (see chapter 18), or use an epoxy glue, and fill the hole completely. Shove the piece of metal into the cavity and position it properly. After the resin or epoxy hardens, trim away any excess around the base of the blade and polish the handle with sandpaper to remove all rough spots *(illustration 12-5)*.

For a knife with the flat sheet of metal for holding the handle, cut an appropriate length of antler about the same width as the metal, secure it in a vise, and with a saw cut it in half lengthways. Position the two halves on either side of the metal and pinch the entire assembly in a vise. Using a drill with a one-eighth-inch bit, bore three

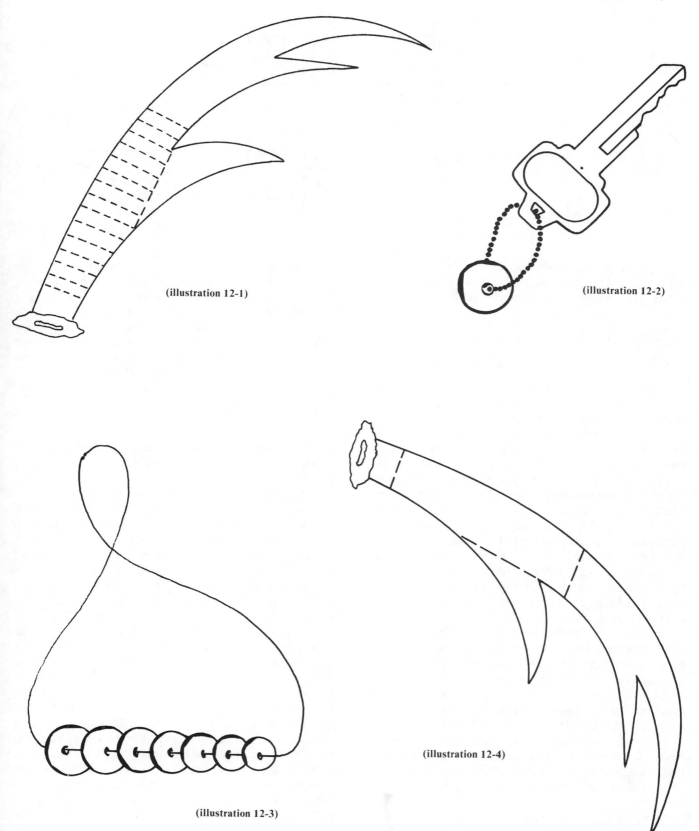

(illustration 12-1)

(illustration 12-2)

(illustration 12-3)

(illustration 12-4)

(illustration 12-5)

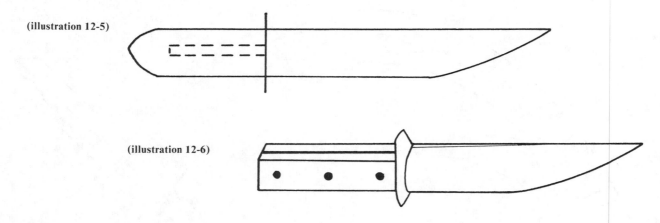

(illustration 12-6)

holes through the handle, one in the middle and the other two each about one-half inch from the ends. Put pieces of one-eighth-inch copper wire through the hole and brad these flat on either side to secure the two halves of bone to the metal band. If any metal protrudes above the bone, grind it flush with the antler. Now polish the antler to remove all rough spots *(illustration 12-6)*.

This basic idea can be applied to many implements and trinkets and any average craftsman can turn out professional-looking creations.

A handle for a bottle opener can be improvised from a piece of antler or tine. Or you might like to make a bottle opener and corkscrew bar set with matching handles.

You might have to buy a bottle opener and remove the handle to substitute one of your own design. Select a piece of antler large enough to accept the implement tang. Again you can use resin or clear epoxy glue. An alternate method is to drill a hole smaller than the tang, boil the antler until the bone begins to soften slightly and drive the tang firmly into the hole. When the antler cools, the implement will be locked permanently into place. Just be sure the hole is deep enough to accept the entire tang *(illustration 12-7)*.

A piece of polished and varnished antler tine—perhaps the so-called brow point of a deer—can be fashioned into a bolo-tie slide, key chain or even a pendant. Cut off a piece of antler tine of correct size and shape and on one side use epoxy glue to anchor the holding slide for a rope bolo tie *(illustration 12-8)*. By drilling a tiny hole in the base of a small piece of tine and adding an appropriate-sized screw eye, you have a key-chain ornament *(illustration 12-9)*. Adapt the same idea for an attractive and unusual necklace pendant, using a much smaller piece of tine and screw eye *(illustration 12-10)*.

Give your imagination a chance and you will come up with numerous ideas. A set of personalized grips for a small pistol can be made from an elk antler *(illustration 12-11)*. Grips for a semi-automatic are easier to make than those for a revolver, but in either case, the job isn't difficult, demanding only a little time. Remove the grips from your favorite handgun to use as a pattern. With a fine-tooth saw cut rough grips approaching the same size, shape and thickness, then use a rasp and sandpaper for final shaping and finishing. Buff to a gloss.

Tusks and Claws

Ideas suggested for antlers can also be applied to tusks, or even to claws from a bobcat, mountain lion or bear.

With a tusk, such as one from a large wild hog or javelina, fill the tooth cavity with epoxy putty (available at most hardware stores) and set a screw eyelet or a square-shouldered staple into the putty before it hardens. The putty dries white. Buff for gloss, varnish, and you have a key chain or necklace ornament.

The claw of a wildcat or bear makes a unique tie clasp, tie tack, necklace pendant or bracelet charm. To remove claws from a dead animal or a fresh skin, make an incision through each toe pad, dissect out the bone to which the claw is attached, and clip it off with tin snips or a diagonal cutter. Put the claws in a can of water for a week or so, or until they slip free. Clean them with an old toothbrush and fill the cavities with clear epoxy, setting a tiny eyelet or U-shaped piece of fine stainless-steel wire into the epoxy, before it dries. The same thing can be done with rattlesnake rattles, first removing the flesh from the base of the rattles and filling with epoxy.

Polished claws or rattles can also be glued to the slide of a bolo tie. Purchase a tie that has an oval or rectangular plastic disk base with a decoration that can be removed. Take off the decoration and replace it with the claw, rattles, or whatever else you choose.

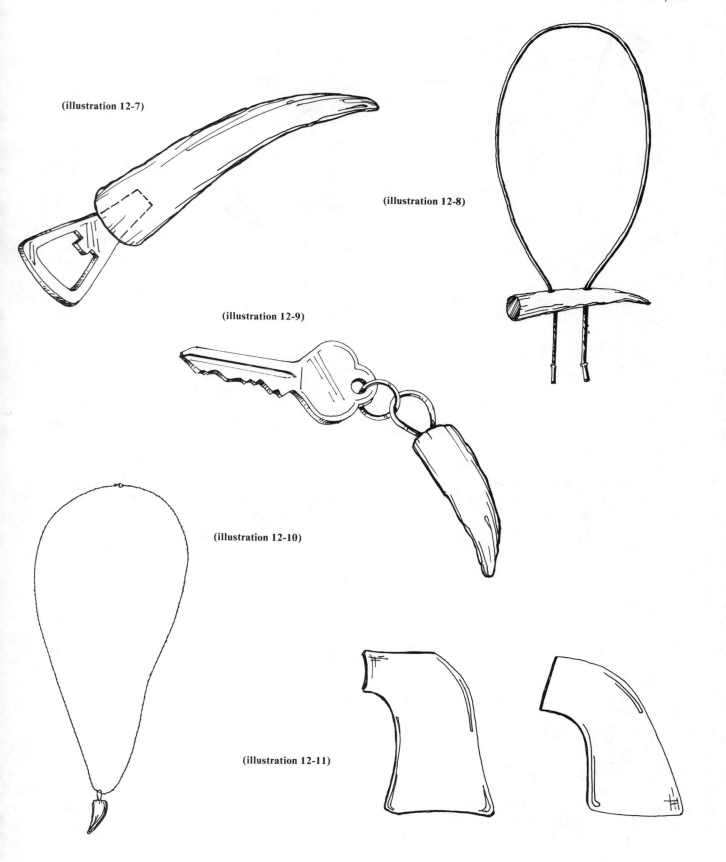

(illustration 12-7)

(illustration 12-8)

(illustration 12-9)

(illustration 12-10)

(illustration 12-11)

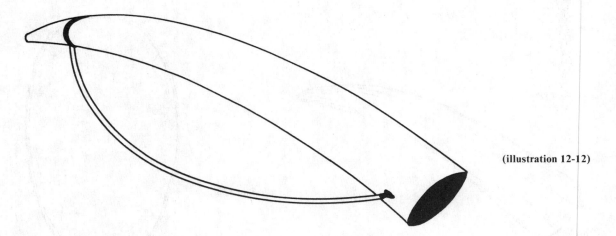

(illustration 12-12)

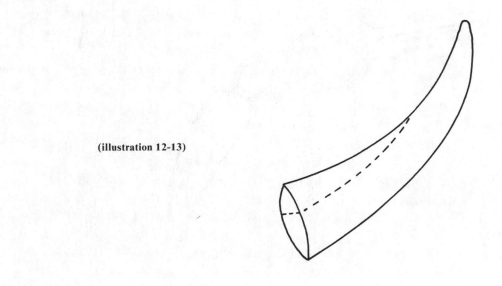

(illustration 12-13)

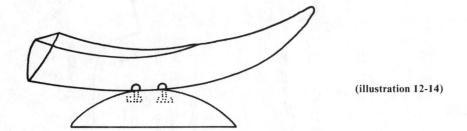

(illustration 12-14)

Horns

All sorts of novel items can be made from cattle horns. Most horns, when polished correctly, have a beautiful luster and color. Perhaps you'll want to mount the horns on a plaque, as described for antlers in chapter 3, or maybe you'd like to make a blowing horn or an ash tray.

To remove the horns from the skull plate, either boil them for 3 or 4 hours, or allow them to soak in cold water for about 2 weeks. Either method will loosen the horns from their cores.

Whatever you intend to make with the horns, they should be polished first. Begin by scraping the horn with a sharp knife to remove all the rough places. On heavy, rough horns it is sometimes necessary to use a rasp. Once the roughness is eliminated, rub the horn with fine sandpaper until it is smooth. To obtain a bright luster, polish with a polishing wheel on an electric drill or motor, using a polishing compound available from a taxidermy supply house (see appendix).

To make a blowing horn, it is best to drill a hole in the solid end rather than to cut off the tip. You'll need all of the tip to fashion a mouthpiece. The easiest way to make this hole is with a piece of No. 9 wire slightly longer than the horn. Bend it to the correct shape to fit inside the horn and extend to the closed tip. Place one end of the wire into flame and get it red hot. Holding the other end with gloves or pliers, run the wire into the horn and burn a hole through the tip. You'll have to keep reheating the wire until it burns completely through.

With a sharp pocketknife, model a mouthpiece around the burned hole. Cut the large end off smooth, far enough back from the tip that the horn isn't too thin. To make a carrying strap, bore a hole in the large end, secure a leather strip with a knot inside, and tie the other end of the strap around the horn near the tip *(illustration 12-7)*.

The tone of the horn can be changed by scraping the horn thinner, using a sharp pocketknife on the outside. The thickness of the bone determines the tone.

For making an ash tray, a small horn is best. Start by cutting a slice off the top *(illustration 12-13)*. Work on the straight side of this slice with sandpaper until it rests flat on the table. Attach the main part of the horn to the slice with two short bolts *(illustration 12-14)*. Be careful not to twist the nuts too tightly or you may crack the bone. If desired, a small strip of aluminum can be bent into the shape of a cigarette holder and mounted on top. There is no need to close the open end, since the natural curve of the horn will cause the ashes to fall back toward the slender, sealed tip.

13/Sculpturing

13/Sculpturing

This chapter might be described as an advanced course for student taxidermists. A professional taxidermist finds sculpturing necessary in his work. What it involves, basically, is molding the head or body of an animal in clay, to its original shape, then taking an impression of this artificial body to be used in making a mannequin. The quality of the mannequin determines whether the animal will appear lifelike when mounted.

Sculpturing can be used in many ways. A professional taxidermist might wish to mount an animal in an attitude—running perhaps—for which no commercial mannequin is available. This means he must design and make his own mannequin. He does this by sculpturing and molding.

The beginner, on the other hand, might like to start from scratch and mount an animal. This involves making everything except the glass eyes. The entire mount then is his own personal accomplishment.

There is nothing easy about sculpturing, no shortcut to success. Much of it you'll learn by trial and error. The sculpturer must possess a certain amount of imagination. When he begins modeling the head from clay, in order to make a mold, he must visualize what the overall subject looks like. He'll get some help from the skull of the animal, but most of it must originate from his own imagination and resourcefulness.

In this chapter the example used is a coyote, a medium-sized animal. While the fundamentals are the same for any creature, large or small, one of medium size—coyote, raccoon, bobcat, fox—is easiest to work with.

Step 1 —*Skinning and Cleaning the Skull*

Commence by skinning the animal for a head mount (see chapter 5). Sever the head from the neck at the base of the skull. Place the flesh-covered skull into a 2-gallon container of boiling water with a teacupful of borax added. Continue to boil for about an hour, or until the flesh separates easily from the bone. Older animals require more boiling than young ones.

Step 2 —*Making the Basic Structure*

While the skull is boiling, measure the length of the animal's neck and the thickness and depth of its shoulders. On a piece of cardboard make a sketch of the shoulder dissection, back as far as you want the mannequin to go. You can get a better idea of the correct size by cutting the neck off at the shoulder.

Scissor out this sketch, place it on the pine board (a piece about 4 inches square and 1 inch thick will do) and

SCULPTURING
(Coyote)

TOOLS
2-gallon bucket
Paintbrush, 1-inch wide
Coping saw
Old kitchen knife
Hammer

SUPPLIES
5 pounds potter's clay or fire clay
20 pounds No. 1 molding plaster
2-foot length of 1- by 8-inch pine board
2 gallons sand
Tin or heavy cardboard
   2 strips 3 inches by 12 inches
   1 strip 3 inches by 8 inches
1 roll of red resin building paper,
   20 pound weight
Excelsior
Small roll twine
12 small shingle nails
Mold separator
1 teacupful 20 Mule Team Borax
Yellow dextrin glue (see appendix)
4 marbles

draw around it. With a coping saw cut out the almost-round chunk of board. This will be the base of the mannequin, or the part of the mount that rests against the wall. Be sure the board isn't too large, since the animal's skin must stretch entirely around it. Now cut a piece of 1- by 2-inch board the length of the neck.

When the flesh will separate from the bone, clean the skull completely of flesh, including brains. Nail the piece of 1- by 2-inch board horizontally into the skull, anchoring it in the brain cavity by driving nails through the sides of the skull into the board. Now nail the base board on the opposite end of the neck board *(illustration 13-1)*.

Position the lower jaw into place (the jaws will separate when the skull is cleaned). If it is to be a closed-mouth mannequin, the simplest to make, bring the jaws together naturally *(illustration 13-2)* and wrap them with string to hold them firmly together. Should you desire an open-mouth mannequin, place a small block of wood in the back of the jaws *(illustration 13-3)* and tie the jaws to-gether with string.

Add excelsior around the 1- by 2-inch board to form the neck *(illustration 13-4)*. The improvised neck should be slightly smaller than the original, since clay will be added over the excelsior.

Step 3 —*Sculpturing*

Mix the clay to a consistency of thick pancake batter. Smear it liberally over the skull and excelsior neck *(illustration 13-5)* and allow it to set for a few minutes, until it begins to harden. Now it can be scraped down to the desired contours, which is much easier than at-tempting to contour with runny clay as you go along. Use a paintbrush dipped in water when you wish to smooth the clay or prevent it from drying too fast.

If it is to be an open-mouth mannequin, the inside of the mouth must be filled with clay, to the outside of the teeth (the teeth will be completely covered with clay). The modeled mouth will have a recess of about one-quarter inch from the outside of the lips *(illustration 13-6)*. When modeling the lips, be sure they do not rise above the teeth, since you desire the teeth to show on the finished mount. On the higher rises of skull, such as the nose and eye sockets, no build-up is necessary; simply brush a light coat of clay over them. The tendency is to get the head too large. Try to keep it as near the exact size of the original head as possible, since the animal's hide must fit over the mannequin later.

Step 4 —*Molding*

Heap the 2 gallons of sand on a large piece of card-

13-1. 1- by 2-inch board goes into the skull and is anchored by driving nails through the sides of the skull into the board. Another piece of board, the size of the coyote's neck, forms the base.

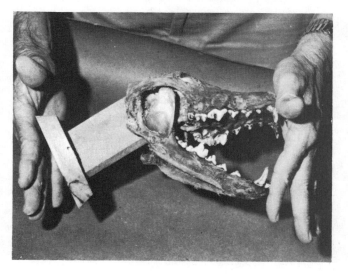

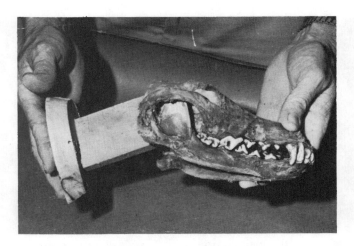

13-2. Bring the jaws together and wrap with string to hold them, if you desire a closed-mouth mount.

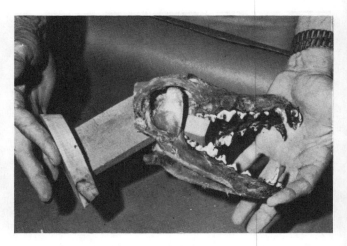

13-3. Should you desire an open-mouth mannequin, put a small piece of board between the jaws to hold them open, then wrap the jaws with string, one or two turns, to hold them in place.

board or a smooth piece of ground or any place that can be cleaned easily later. Moisten the sand to make it easier to work with.

It is simpler to use sand this way rather than in a box, since you can tell exactly when the skull is buried to the desired depth. Dig a depression in the sand and place the clayed skull into it, putting a chunk of board along the back to form the base of the mold (put some sand behind the board to give it support). Bury the skull exactly halfway down, employing a small block of wood to pat the sand smooth *(illustration 13-7)*.

Take the three strips of tin or heavy cardboard and build a makeshift fence around the skull, pushing the strips down into the sand and putting some sand behind them for support, so the weight of the poured plaster won't tilt them over *(illustration 13-8)*. Place four marbles halfway into the sand, two on top and two on bottom of the buried skull *(illustration 13-8)*. These marbles will help align the two mold halves later.

Mix the plaster to a consistency of thick whipped cream and pour it over the entire sculptured skull. Remember that plaster hardens quickly and should be poured immediately after it is mixed *(illustration 13-9)*. Check to make sure that the entire skull is covered *(illustration 13-10)*.

Allow the plaster to set for a few minutes, then add another coat. On larger molds, strips of burlap dipped in plaster and placed between each two coats will give the finished mold strength. Use three or four coats of plaster, until the plaster is several inches thick.

After the plaster has hardened thoroughly (about 30 minutes), gingerly turn the mold, leaving the skull in place, and rest it in the depression of sand. Wash it lightly with water to remove all particles of sand, scraping

the sand away where necessary. Paint the edges of raw plaster with clay, covering completely; this will form a separator when the two halves are taken apart later. Remove the four marbles and paint the cavities with clay. When both halves of the mold are completed, this will result in four small knobs and four recesses of identical size. When the knobs and recesses are fitted together, the two halves will be aligned perfectly.

Use the strips of tin or cardboard to build a fencework again, using sand on the outside to support it. This prevents the plaster from running. Now pour the plaster over this side, as you did on the other, adding several coats and pieces of burlap if necessary for strength.

After the mold is hard, take an old kitchen knife and gently force it into the crack which separates the two molds and pry the halves apart. Remove the skull and wash the mold thoroughly, to eliminate all sand *(illustration 13-11)*. The two halves of the mold *(illustration 13-12)* will be used for making the mannequin.

If you want to preserve the teeth for an open-mouth mannequin, clean all the clay from the mouth and saw out the teeth, about one-half inch above and below. (Artificial teeth available from a taxidermy supply house can be substituted if necessary.) The rest of the skull can be thrown away.

Step 5 —*Making the Mannequin*

Rub the inside of each mold thoroughly with separator (see Appendix). Use a cloth to wipe out all excess.

To make the mannequin you'll need red resin building paper in 20-pound weight, available in a large roll from

13-4. Excelsior is compressed around the 1- by 2-inch board to form the neck, with the excelsior neck being slightly smaller than the original neck.

any lumberyard. One roll will make a number of mannequins. Also needed is yellow dextrin glue, which can be ordered from a taxidermy supply house and is also available at some drugstores.

The glue comes in powdered form and will need some preparation. Mix equal parts of flour and glue in cold water, to the consistency of pancake batter. After it is thoroughly mixed, add enough water to thin it considerably, place it in a container over heat and cook, stirring constantly, until it becomes a thick paste.

Now for the actual making of the mannequin. Tear the paper in small strips, smear them lightly with glue, and place the strips in the mold *(illustration 13-13)*, completely covering the entire inside to a thickness of about five layers of paper. Rub each layer down firmly, to eliminate any air bubbles.

After both molds have been covered adequately with paper, place the halves together, one on top of the other.

13-5. Clay is spread over the excelsior and contoured to resemble the coyote's original neck.

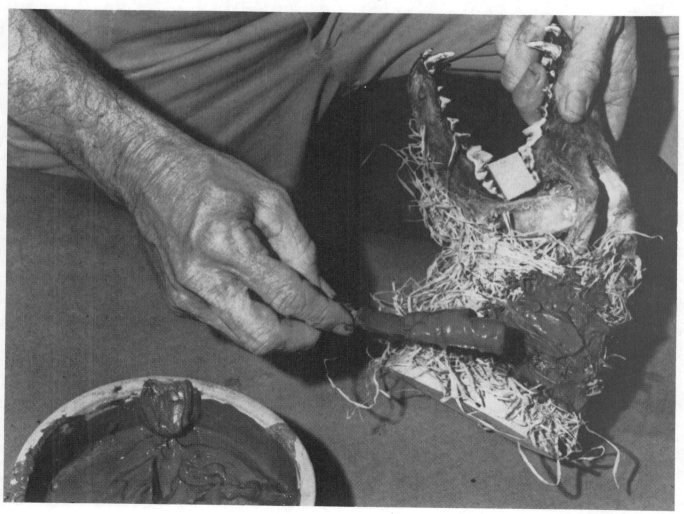

Take other glue-covered strips of paper and reach inside the mold, through the hole in the back, and cover the cracks between the molds all the way around to a thickness of five layers of paper.

If you are making a mannequin for an antlered or horned animal, you will, at this stage, need to add a block of wood inside the head, against the top of the skull. Cut a piece of pine board about the size of the skull plate and, reaching inside the mold, position it at the top of the head and anchor it firmly with two or three strips of glue-covered paper. This board is necessary for anchoring the skull plate with the antlers or horns attached.

Allow the mannequin to dry for 24 hours. Now gently lift the top side of the mold away and you have a rough

mannequin *(illustration 13-14)*. Remove the mannequin, dip your hands in glue and rub the substance lightly over the entire form. This coat of glue will later act as a bond between hide and mannequin. The seam on the outside, where the molds came together, will be exposed. Take a single strip of paper, coat it with glue, and press it over the seam. Now you have a finished mannequin *(illustration 13-15)*. Allow the finished mannequin to dry thoroughly, which will require 5 or 6 days under normal weather conditions.

The same mold can be used to make a urethane form or mannequin. Urethane is comprised of two chemicals that, when mixed in equal parts, produce an immediate reaction, expanding and turning into a rigid, rubber-like plastic. Urethane can be obtained from industrial chem-

13-6. For an open-mouth mannequin, the inside of the mouth must be filled with clay to the outside of the teeth, covering the teeth completely with clay.

13-7. The clay-covered head is half buried in sand and the sand smoothed by a small block of wood.

13-8. A makeshift fence is built from strips of tin or cardboard around the clay head, and the four marbles are pushed halfway into the sand as shown.

13-9. Plaster is mixed and poured over the clay head.

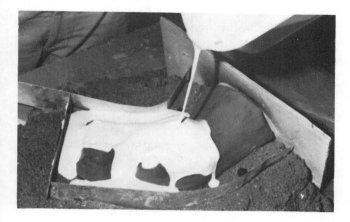

13-10. If the head isn't entirely covered with a thick layer of plaster, give it another application.

13-11. When the plaster hardens, turn so that the exposed half of the clay skull is up. Remove the four marbles and coat the four recesses and the edges of raw plaster with a light covering of clay to act as a separator. Now pour plaster over the exposed half of the skull.

ical stores or ordered from a taxidermy supply house (see Appendix). A word of caution, however: you must have everything ready and be prepared to work quickly, because once the two chemicals are mixed together the whole process will be over in 15 minutes or less.

As the urethane expands, it creates tremendous pressure—especially when the mold cavity has filled up while the expansion is still going on. Because expansion is about five times the amount of mixed liquid poured into the mold, the tendency at first is to mix too much urethane. Unless there is a way for the excess material to escape, pressure will build until it blows the mold apart. Even veteran taxidermists have this happen to them occasionally.

Small forms are the easiest to make; and fish forms are simpler than animals. Big game shoulder mounts should not be attempted, unless you have a fiberglass mold designed and made to take a lot of stress from urethane. Fiberglass molds, which are expensive, require locking bolts along the edge to hold the two halves securely together. It is much easier to buy such big game forms from a supply house.

The smallest amount of urethane mix you can buy is one gallon (making two gallons total). That quantity will make a lot of small mannequins, more than you probably will ever use—another reason why it's cheaper to order the type forms you need from a supply house.

Now, let's get to work. Clean both halves of the mold cavities thoroughly, then coat them liberally with petroleum jelly, which is the release agent *(illustration 13-16)*. The mold will absorb some of the petroleum jelly; if any dry spots are left, the urethane will stick and you'll have to tear it loose, damaging the mannequin. After the mold sets for a few minutes, wipe off any excess petroleum jelly with a dry cloth.

Anchor the two sides of the mold together *(illustration 13-17)*, using something similar to these homemade clamps. You can also wrap the mold with a small chain, but be sure to use a few wedges of wood under the chain to eliminate slack and keep the expanding urethane from forcing the two halves apart. You can also wrap the mold tightly with a couple layers of duct tape. In any event, it's very important to prevent the sides from separating as a result of internal pressure.

In order to hang the coyote head mount on a wall, you'll need a board attached to the neck. Cut and shape one to fit *(illustration 13-18)*. First, pour equal amounts of the urethane chemicals into two foam plastic cups (a coffee cup about half full of each is enough). In this trial-and-error process, you need to avoid more expansion than the mold can hold. If the mold doesn't fill with the first chemical, mix and add a small amount (if a small blemish or two appears because the mold didn't fill completely, these can be repaired with plaster or papier-mache).

Pour the two chemicals together into a larger container and stir vigorously for a few seconds to mix. Then immediately pour the chemical into the mold *(illustration 13-19)*. Watch the urethane expand. As it nears the top,

place the shaped board into the neck and put a larger board over it *(illustration 13-20)* to hold it in place. As the urethane pushes against the board, use all your strength to apply enough pressure to keep the urethane confined in the mold.

13-12. When you are finished and the skull is removed, you will have a mold as shown.

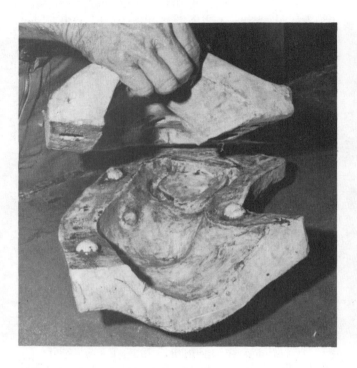

13-13. You build the mannequin by tearing the red resin paper into strips and smearing each one lightly with glue before placing it into the mold.

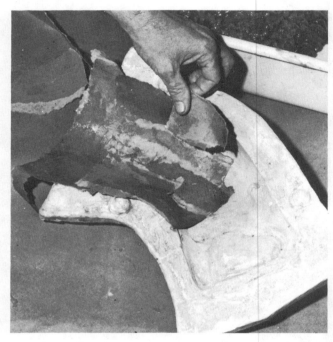

13-14. When the job is completed, you will have a mannequin like this.

13-15. For final finishing, rub a light application of glue over the entire mannequin and glue a strip of paper over the seam where the two halves of the mold came together.

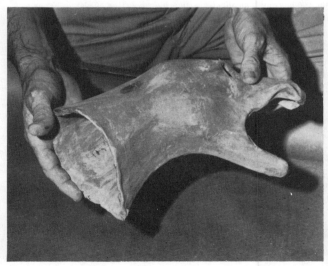

Once expansion stops, wait for about 10 more minutes for the plastic to harden. Take out the rough form *(illustration 13-21)* and, using a sharp knife, trim off all the rough edges *(illustration 13-22)*. All that's needed now is to cut out the mouth so that the teeth can be positioned in place. You may now proceed to the mounting of the coyote head *(illustration 13-23)*.

Step 6 —*Mounting*

If it is an open-mouth mannequin, add the teeth (see section "Rug with Mounted Head", in chapter 10). Then the head can be mounted (chapter 5). When you are

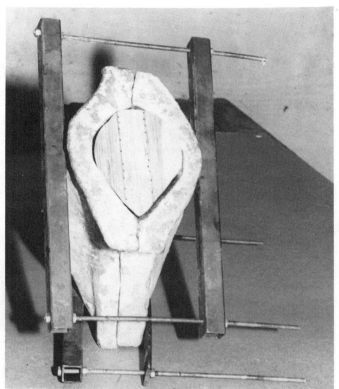

13-18. Cut and shape a board to fit.

13-19. Immediately after combining the two chemicals, pour the mixture into the mold.

13-16. Coat both halves of the mold liberally with petroleum jelly.

13-17. Use clamps (similar to these homemade examples) to anchor the two sides together.

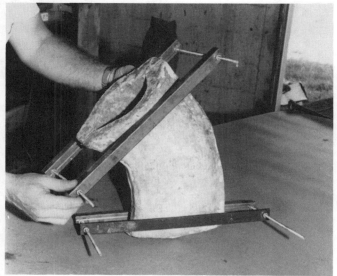

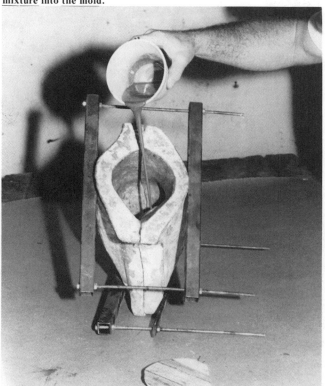

finished, you have a mount *(illustration 13-23)* that is entirely the result of your own imagination and skill.

More on Mannequin Making

Modeling and casting constitute only one method of creating a finished mannequin. You can also make one mannequin from another.

If you have the space, you can store the molds, marking them as to size and type, and use them again and again. This is what professional taxidermists do, building a "library" of mannequin molds.

The simplest method is merely to build one mannequin from another. Suppose you want a mannequin to mount a deer head. Buy the next size smaller than the head, add clay all over for the finished sculpturing and you are ready to make a mold. Don't forget the block of wood in head for attaching skull plate, *(illustration 13-24)*.

Most taxidermists do not like to copy other people's works. Some taxidermy supply outlets which sell mannequins forbid copies. But Lem Rathbone does not mind having his mannequins copied.

"If someone goes to all this work—sculpturing and casting—he has earned the right to copy one of my mannequins," Rathbone says. "And his own individual creative art will be expressed if he takes the time and effort to make his mannequin different from someone else's."

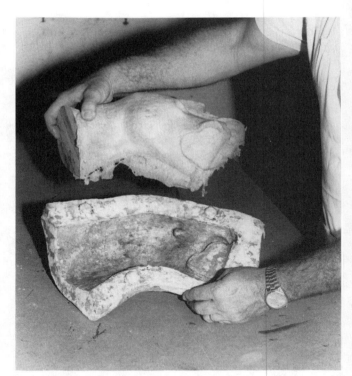

13-21. After the plastic has hardened, remove the rough form.

13-22. Trim off the rough edges with a sharp knife.

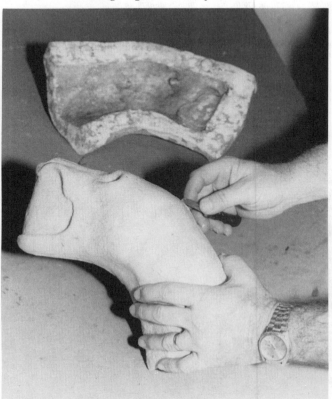

13-20. Hold the shaped board in place with a larger board.

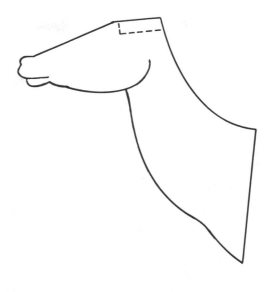

13-23. Here is the final mount, with the coyote cape put on the mannequin you made.

13-24. Shaded area shows where the block of wood goes into the mannequin to provide an anchor for attaching antlers or horns.

Many things can be done to alter a mannequin. You can make it larger or smaller, turn the head, or change the general shape altogether.

Suppose you would like a deer-head mannequin facing slightly to the right rather than straight ahead. Make or buy a straight-on mannequin a size smaller than the head. Decide where the turn of the neck should be and cut out the amount you think needs changing. This might be 2 or 3 inches, or as much as 6 inches. Saw the mannequin at both ends of the section and remove it.

Take heavy wire or maybe thin pieces of board (using nails) and utilize this to replace the removed section temporarily, turning the head in the direction and to the angle desired. Use papier-mâché or plaster to fill the hole where the section was removed. Once this filler hardens, the wire or board supports can be removed.

Cover with clay, as previously described, make a plaster cast and you have another mold. It is fun to make these alterations and see how they turn out. No two taxidermists see a deer head in exactly the same way. The tilt or angle may be different, or one may want to turn the head more than another would.

You can make a smaller mannequin by using a larger one, taking out sections, putting it back together, using papier-mâché or plaster when necessary, sculpturing with clay and casting to make a mold. However, it is easier to increase—taking a smaller mannequin and building it up—than to reduce the size.

You might ruin a mannequin or two as you experiment, but if you have a mold to make your own, you can create another with a little time, work and nominal outlay for materials.

14/Tanning

14/Tanning

If you take a hide to be tanned to a taxidermist, who in turn ships it to a commercial tannery, when you eventually pick up the finished product you probably will consider the price a bit steep, since you furnished the skin and paid only for a service. But attempt the job yourself at home, and you will probably wonder how a tannery can do the work so cheaply.

Make no mistake, home tanning is an arduous, time-consuming, exasperating job. Moreover, you are likely not to be pleased with the way the do-it-yourself project turns out. The tannery does a much better job because it has precision machinery to accomplish the two most difficult chores, shaving and finishing. The hide is run through a shaving machine to clean it and give uniform thickness. Thicker hides, such as that of a bull, might split into two or three layers. Some hides are then dumped into a large motor-driven drum partly filled with sawdust. Humidity is rigidly controlled. The hides are tumbled inside the drum—the action pulling and stretching them—until the tanning process is completed.

After being forewarned, if you still want to try home tanning, the instructions follow.

Home tanning was not included in the first edition of this book, because of the difficulty of finding the necessary chemicals, particularly if you live in a small community. But now there are home tanning kits

(illustration 14-1) which contain all the chemicals you will need. Such kits are available from either of the following sources:

Austin Taxidermist Studio
8739 Highway 290 West
Austin, Texas 78737

Van Dyke Supply
Woonsocket, South Dakota 57385

If you want to collect the ingredients yourself, you will need salt, alum and borax. If you wish to make buckskin rather than tan the hide with the hair on, you will also need hydrated lime and boric acid.

Tanning solutions are also made from phenol or sulfuric acid, caustic solutions which I do not recommend because of the risks involved, or from tannic acid, which is almost impossible to obtain in small amounts.

There are several types of alum available, but chrome alum seems to give the most satisfactory results. You can probably get it from a chemical company or a taxidermy supply house. On dry skins, such as those of deer, you also should use neat's-foot oil or a special tanning oil (from a taxidermy supply outlet). The oil makes

TANNING

TOOLS
Plastic trash can
Currier's knife or sharp butcher knife

SUPPLIES
Home-tanning kit, or the following:
Salt
Alum
20 Mule Team Borax
Lead-free gasoline
Neat's-foot oil

ADDITIONAL SUPPLIES FOR
HAIR-OFF BUCKSKIN
Hydrated lime
Boric acid

14-1. Tanning kits come complete with all the ingredients you need for a home tanning job.

the tanned skin more pliable and provides some resistance against moisture. Greasy skins, such as those of bears, should be given a quick soaking in lead-free gasoline, then hung and allowed to drain.

Aluminum sulfate can be substituted for alum, and in some ways it does a better job, producing a softer leather with less shrinkage. The problem with this solution, however, is that it also calls for a small amount of gambier or terra japonica, neither of which may be readily available. Try a drugstore, a chemical house or maybe a taxidermist.

The following solutions will suffice for soaking a deer hide. If you would rather experiment with a much smaller hide, which will also be thinner, and on both counts easier to tan, cut the amounts of all ingredients in half.

Alum and salt solution: Mix 1 pound alum and 2 pounds salt in 4 gallons water (soft water if possible), stirring until the chemicals are completely dissolved.

Aluminum sulfate solution: Mix 2 pounds aluminum sulfate (iron free) and 2 pounds salt in 2 gallons warm, soft water until dissolved. In a separate container dissolve 6 ounces gambier or terra japonica in 2 quarts of water. Mix the two liquids thoroughly and add enough water to make 4 gallons of solution.

Obtain all the ingredients before you start. There is no need to mix a solution until you are ready for it, but should you need to store a mixed solution for even a short time, do not put it in a metal container, which will corrode. Plastic containers are much better. If you can't find one large enough, gallon-sized plastic milk jugs will do.

Before you need the solution, there is much work to be done. How the hide is prepared will determine to a great extent how the finished product will turn out.

Step 1 —*Curing the Hide*

You can tan a fresh or green hide, but it is much better to salt-cure the hide properly. Not only does salting halt bacterial action that would loosen the hair and spoil the hide, but the flesh side of the hide is much easier to shave after it has been salt-cured.

Rub a heavy layer of common table salt completely over the flesh side of the hide, making sure you get the salt into every crease and corner. Use non-iodized salt. Do not use rock salt because the large granules may not dehydrate the skin uniformly.

The salted hide should be put in a cool, shady spot for a few days—long enough to cure properly yet not so long as to become hard and dry. Should it become hard, soak it in water until it becomes soft again. How long this will take depends on the dryness and thickness of the hide. When it becomes soft, remove from the water and hang to drain, but don't leave it so long that it becomes hard again.

Step 2 —*Shaving*

This is a painstaking job that will take some time, especially if you have never done it before. A shaving board *(illustration 14-2)* can be built to accommodate the job. If you have a small hide, such as that of a raccoon, you can make a miniature model of the board and nail or clamp to a table *(illustration 14-3)*.

A currier's knife with two sharp replaceable blades with turned-down edges is designed specifically for this shaving, but you can use an ordinary butcher knife, if it is very sharp and large enough that you can grasp the handle with one hand and the back side of the blade near the point with the fingers of the other. Or, you can hammer a block of wood over the point for a makeshift handle, giving you a handle at each end. Whichever method you pick, do not attempt to apply too much pressure as you shave. If you push too hard you will probably cut through the skin and the slash will show on the tanned hide. Always cut away from your body *(illustration 14-4)*.

Shave off fat and any thick, hard spots. The cleaner you get the hide the better the tanning job. Try if possible to obtain uniform thickness all over. Trim the ragged edges into smooth lines.

Step 3 —*Removing the Hair*

(If you prefer to tan the hide with the hair on, omit this step.)

Make a solution by mixing 1 pound of hydrated lime

14-2. A heavy-duty shaving board. You can improvise one from almost any lumber you can find.

14-3. A smaller shaving board like this can be nailed or clamped to a table.

into about 1 gallon of warm water, stirring until the chemical is dissolved. Then add extra liquid to have 4 gallons of solution. A large plastic trash can or tub makes a good container. Remember, never use metal containers for any tanning solution.

Rinse the hide in cool water several times to remove the salt and any dirt. Let it drain. Now submerge it in the lime solution. You may have to weight it with a brick or two to keep it completely submerged. Stir it two or three times each day so that the lime solution will penetrate every area. In a week or more the lime should have done its duty and the hair will commence to slip. Leave it long enough so that all hair is completely loose. Now remove it from the solution, put it over the fleshing board, hair up, and with a dull knife scrape off the hair. If the hair does not come off easily and cleanly, put the hide back in the solution and soak it for a few more days.

When the hair has come off, rinse the hide again in warm water to remove the lime, replacing the water two or three times. Mix 4 ounces of boric acid in 4 gallons of water and submerge the hide again. This solution neutralizes any remaining lime. Soak about a day, remove and rinse.

Step 4 —*The Tanning Solution*

Mix either the alum or the aluminum sulfate solution in a plastic container. Do this while the hide is draining. If you put it into the tanning solution immediately after rinsing it, the excess water trapped in the hide will dilute the solution, making it less effective.

The hide must be kept in the tanning solution for a week or more, depending on its size and thickness. If possible, maintain the solution at normal room temperature. Keep in mind that it is better to leave the hide in the solution longer than necessary than to remove it before the solution has soaked through completely.

Examine the hide periodically to see if the flesh side has turned white. If it has, cut off a tiny piece, the thickest part you can find along the edges, to determine whether the hide is white all the way through. If you have any doubt, leave it a day or so longer in the solution as insurance.

By this point a lot of time has been spent, but the task is far from finished. One reason for using a tanning kit is that it saves time. You don't have to run around looking for all the ingredients. Some kits—the Lawrence Professional Home Tanning Kit, for example—also contains a rapid tan pickling and tanning compound, which needs only to be mixed with water and cuts the soaking time about in half.

When the hide is taken from the pickling solution, rinse it first in a water-borax mix, 1 ounce of borax per gallon of water, then rinse with plain water and hang to drain. As an alternative squeeze out as much water as you can by hand, but do not wring the hide. The skin should be damp but not wet.

Lay it on a smooth surface, flesh side up, and apply the neat's-foot oil or tanning oil. Pour on small amounts and rub in with your fingers, or use a cloth or sponge. About 4 ounces of oil will suffice for an ordinary deer hide. Once it is oiled all over, roll it up, the flesh or oiled side in, and leave it overnight.

Step 5 —*Finishing*

Budget a full day for this. As the hide dries, it must be stretched to soften. You can do this by pulling it back

14-4. When shaving a hide, always cut away from your body.

and forth over the end of the shaving board *(illustration 14-5)* or over the top of an upright post. The more pulling and stretching you do, the softer the final product will be. If it isn't pulled enough, the skin will dry hard and stiff.

How long this finishing requires will depend on how steadily and vigorously you pull and stretch the hide. Assuming that you stop occasionally to rest, it will take at least several hours. Keep pulling and stretching in all directions until the hide is fully dry and soft.

If for any reason you have to leave the finishing for a time, the hide must be again soaked in water and re-oiled, and the pulling and stretching started over from the beginning.

Periodically, when you pause to rest, it is a good idea to go over the flesh side of the hide lightly with a sponge soaked in neat's-foot oil. This helps to make the skin softer.

You will probably be disappointed with your first ef-fort. Most beginners don't leave the hide in the pickling solution long enough or are haphazard with the finishing—not pulling and stretching the hide sufficiently. With no exceptions, the output (the quality of the finished product) is in direct ratio to the input (the time and effort spent in the complete process).

Read this chapter several times before undertaking the job. Make sure that you understand each step and have all the necessary ingredients. If you use a home-tanning kit, read the instructions carefully. Each has a slightly different procedure. No step can be by-passed, except for removing the hair.

You have been forewarned this is a tough and laborious job, a messy undertaking that demands a lot of time. Unlike making a mount, which you can progressively watch take shape, with tanning you have no feeling of accomplishment until the job is completed. But tanning is also a challenge. Anyone who tans a hide at home successfully can be justifiably proud.

14-5. With a small hide, such as this rabbit skin, the stretching and drying processes take much less time and effort.

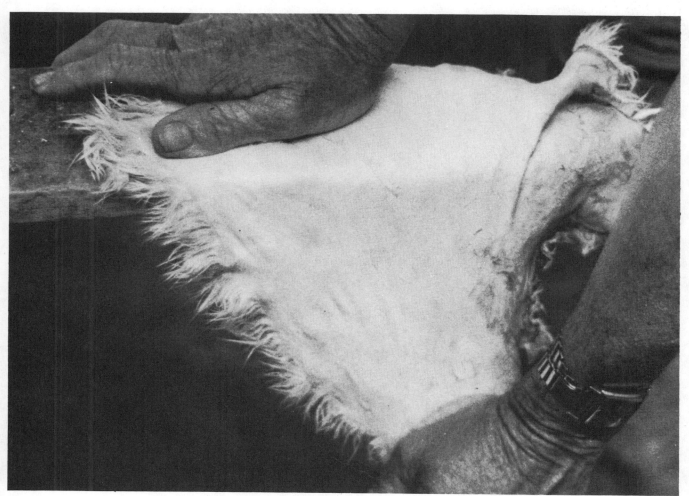

15/Lifelike Snakes

15/Lifelike Snakes

In basic procedure a snake mount is similar to the plastic fish described in chapter 3, but it is a little more complex and requires greater imagination because you must arrange the snake in a lifelike pose, exactly as it will appear when the mount is finished.

To begin with, you must have a live snake, which complicates the matter. Either catch one yourself or obtain one from another source. If the snake is a venomous one, handle it with extreme care.

The snake must be killed in such a way that it suffers no damage—you want no flaws to appear in the mount. There are two ways to do this; either by using chloroform (available from most drugstores) or by freezing. Rathbone prefers chloroform.

For the chloroform method, take a container that is virtually airtight, such as a box with a tight lid. Place the snake inside, pour in about an ounce of chloroform, close the lid, and leave it be for about an hour. Before removing the snake, poke it with a stick and watch for any sign of life. Snakes that appear dead have been known to bite.

For the freeze method, which many taxidermists prefer, put the reptile into a freezer, wait until it is solid and quite dead, then thaw the body.

But, again, be very cautious. Bob Herndon of Aransas Pass, Texas, who specializes in snake taxidermy, has handled thousands of venomous snakes. Yet one lapse in caution almost cost him his life. He picked up a big Western diamondback rattlesnake which he thought was frozen and dead. In fact, the tail end was frozen. But what happened, probably, was that the reptile had buried its head among other snakes put into the freezer at the same time, and that end remained active. The snake turned suddenly and buried its fangs deep into Herndon's arm. Only because he knew what to do in such an emergency did Herndon save the limb, and perhaps his life.

When the dead snake has become limber, arrange it on a piece of plywood or a sheet of glass that is large enough to hold the coiled reptile yet small enough to fit into the freezer. Crumble some heavy paper into a ball about the size of a softball. You may need to press this down some when you begin working with the snake. Coil the snake around this ball to make the middle rise above the sides, which will look more lifelike.

When you have it in a coil, use cotton balls to adjust the position, maybe packing balls around the head to make it stand up and arch back, as if the snake were ready to strike. Use all the cotton you need for support, since the balls are removed later. Take your time and be sure the snake is arranged as perfectly as you can get it. This is the most important step, since it will determine

LIFELIKE SNAKE

TOOLS
Tiny fine-hair paintbrush

SUPPLIES
Chloroform
Piece of plywood
Small ball of heavy paper
Cotton balls
Molding plaster
P-300 rubber compound
Resin and catalyst (hardener) paraffin
Glass eyes
Paint

the kind of finished mount you will ultimately make.

If you are working with a rattlesnake, remove the rattles by cutting them off where they join the body. Save the rattles. No alteration is needed on any other species.

Place the board with the snake on it in the freezer, being careful as not to change the arrangement. Let the snake freeze solid *(illustration 15-1)*.

Before removing it, have molding plaster ready (just as when making a plastic fish). Take the snake out and remove all the cotton balls but leave the reptile on the board. The ball of paper is hidden and frozen inside. With a hose, rinse the snake, eliminating all frost. While it is still wet, cover it completely with plaster. Use enough to make a good strong mold.

Allow the plaster to harden. By then the snake will be unfrozen and limp. Carefully pull it out of the mold. Some of the feather edges on the bottom may chip away, but this will be on the hidden part of the mount and won't show. Now put the mold in a dry place and allow

15-1. This rattler was arranged in a sleeping pose and frozen before it was covered with plaster to make a mold.

it to cure. Give it at least 10 days. This is very important because the dry plaster absorbs moisture from the rubber compound which is poured into it next, pulling the rubber tight against the mold sides to accent every feature, and also causing the rubber to harden.

For the next step you will need some P-300 rubber compound. This looks like milk and has about the same consistency. You should be able to get it from one of the larger taxidermy supply houses (see Appendix). Buy at least 2 quarts. One quart will suffice for most average-sized snakes, but it is better to have too much rather than too little, and you can save the excess for later use.

When the mold is completely dry, turn it upside down and use some objects, such as rocks or books, to hold it steady and level. Pour the rubber compound into the mold until it is full.

As the mold absorbs the moisture, the level of the rubber compound will drop slightly. About every 2 hours replenish the compound, bringing it back to full. The rubber will harden only next to the mold, a thickness of about one-eighth inch. After about 12 hours, pour any excess rubber back into the bottle for later use. Leave the mold overnight. There will be a little shrinkage as the rubber hardens completely.

You now have a rubber snake, which is hollow in the center. If you are careful, you can pull it out of the mold, but it is better to take a hammer and break the mold away. No harm is done if you accidentally hit the snake.

The next step is to melt about a pint of paraffin, turn the rubber snake upside down, support it with something to keep it steady and level, and pour the paraffin into the cavity. This keeps the rubber snake uniform in size and makes it appear more lifelike.

The paraffin-filled rubber snake should be allowed to cure for 4 or 5 days. There will be a small amount of shrinkage, and if you paint it too soon, this will cause the paint to crack.

If you are using a rattlesnake, trim the edge of the rattles and the snake's tail until they are smooth. Then stick one end of a short piece of stiff wire into the rattles and the other end into the snake. Fill the crack between the two with resin mixed with hardener. This will give a permanent bond.

For painting you can use either common oil paint or lacquer (but don't mix the two). Get a color photograph of the snake species, determine the basic color, and with an aerosol can spray a light coat over the entire snake.

Once this dries, you are ready to add the glass eyes. Cut out the eye sockets, making the holes large enough to accept the eyes. Place the eyes in the proper position and anchor them with resin.

The final finishing is done with a tiny fine-hair brush and paints of appropriate colors. For a quality job you need to paint each scale individually. This is a tedious job, but the time and effort are well spent. A sloppy paint job will ruin the entire project.

15-2. As these photographs of a live rattlesnake show (see also next page), a snake's poses can vary. Arrange the dead snake in a manner which appears realistic to you, using cotton balls liberally. Stand back periodically to see what changes will give the snake a more "alive" look.

16/Care of Mounts

16/Care of Mounts

A dirty mount suggests that the owner does not have enough pride in his trophy to keep it in the best of condition. While an "average" mount, if it is clean and tidy, looks pretty good to the casual observer, even the best quality mount will appear shoddy and "flat" when it is soiled.

Regular upkeep is necessary. Dust off the trophy occasionally with a soft rag or a feather duster. In time, however, an accumulation of grime and dust prompts a more thorough cleaning. How often this is required depends on periodical upkeep, but every mount should have a complete cleaning at least every two years, perhaps oftener.

Big-Game Head Mounts

About every month or so take a damp rag and rub the trophy down thoroughly, pushing the cloth with the hair—not against it, which tends to break the hair. When you are through cleaning, brush the hair to make it lie naturally.

To remove dust, employ a soft rag or a feather duster. *Do not* use a vacuum cleaner. The suction ruffles the hair and breaks it off.

If a mount is badly soiled, select a hot summer day for cleaning. Remove the mount from the wall and place it where you can scrub it down. The drainboard of the kitchen sink will do. Dissolve some powdered detergent in cool water, the amount of soap depending on how dirty the mount is. Use a brush with soft bristles and thoroughly saturate the hair of the mount, brushing with the hair. Afterward, take the mount outdoors and rinse it with a garden hose. Use only a moderate amount of water pressure to avoid breaking the ears or getting water into the ears and between the hide and the mannequin.

Comb and brush the mount thoroughly. This removes excess water and straightens the hair; if it is crooked it will dry that way. Hang the mount in the sun for several days, or until it is thoroughly dry.

Mounts of antlered animals need to have the antlers "fed" about every other year. To do this, saturate a rag in boiled (not raw) linseed oil. Go over the antlers thoroughly with the oily rag, and afterwards take a dry cloth and rub all the excess oil away. The antlers will appear greasy when you are finished, but in a few days the bone will absorb all the oil. This oiling makes the antlers look fresh again, rather than bleached out. Horned animals, however, do not need oil; in fact, oil placed on the horns of any wild sheep mount will ruin them. Sheep horns have natural oils and any added oil

16-1. Holes are bored in the broken antler and a pin is inserted.

discolors the bone.

Periodically, every big-game head mount will need another paint job on the nose and around the nostrils and eyes, to restore the slick, lifelike look.

Should an antlered mount fall or be dropped and a tine (point) breaks, the broken part can be restored. Retrieve all the parts possible and position the broken tine back on the main antler beam to determine how it will fit. Bone seldom breaks evenly and you'll probably have nicks and holes where small bits of the antler are missing. Take a drill, the size of the bit depending on how large the antler is, and drill a hole about 1 inch deep, if possible, through the parts to be fastened together. Into this hole insert some sort of pin, maybe a length of nail (see drawing, 16-1). The holes should be slightly larger than the pin so that an adhesive substance can be packed into the hole on both parts of the broken antler. After you get the two parts fitted back together as naturally as possible (with the pin inside), mix a small amount of resin, catalyst and shredded asbestos (see appendix). Pull the break apart and put some of this substance into the holes drilled for the pin; then reinsert the pin and position the antler in place. With more of the paste-like resin and asbestos, fill in around the crack,

modeling the nicks and cracks. Some surplus should completely cover the cracks. After allowing the resin to harden for several days, take an electric sander and sand the antler back to its original shape, removing all surplus resin and smoothing the surface. Leave a film of hard resin thick enough to obscure the break completely. Unless the antler is scrutinized closely, the break will be impossible to detect.

Birds

About the only maintenance for bird mounts is to dust them off occasionally. Use either a soft, dry cloth or wadded cotton, brushing with the lay of the feathers at all times. Never use a vacuum cleaner or a damp cloth. Suction breaks the feathers and moisture will ruin them. When the mount gets dull, repaint the bill and feet.

Fish

When cleaning fish mounts, use a damp cloth or sponge to wipe the dirt away. If the finish gets dull, go over it with a coat of clear white shellac. This makes the fish slick and shiny again. Shellac is recommended because it can be used over either varnish or lacquer bases. If lacquer is put over a varnish base, it will ruin the original paint job.

A crack in the fin or tail can be repaired by putting a small piece of tissue paper over the crack on the back side and covering the paper completely with clear fingernail polish. This glues the paper to the fin or tail and prevents it from tearing again.

Should the crack be gaping, mix clear fingernail polish and cotton to obtain a substance about the consistency of putty. Fill up the crack, modeling the substance smoothly so that the fin or tail will appear natural when it dries.

Whole-Animal Mounts

The mount of any animal with fur can be washed and brushed and dried in the same way as a big-game head mount. Leave it in the sunshine to dry thoroughly.

17/The Taxidermy Knife

17/The Taxidermy Knife

The most important tool in the taxidermist's shop is probably his knife. It should feel natural in your hands, with a comfortable handle and a blade of a length and thickness that works best for you. One man's fillet knife is another man's skinning knife, but for most jobs a shorter blade (4 to 5 inches) is easier to manage. A medium-sized kitchen butcher knife will do the job just fine. Above all, the knife must have a prepared cutting edge that will last. According to John Juranitch, a professional sharpening consultant and author of *The Razor Edge Book of Sharpening* (see Appendix for ordering copies), the accuracy of the cut depends largely on the edge, whether the knife is used for surgery, butchering or taxidermy.

"You can be certain of one problem," Juranitch adds. "Whatever knife you choose, it will have poor *relief (illustration 17-1)*. Relief is the area of thickness (or thinness, as the case may be) located directly behind the cutting edge. Good relief guarantees a blade that's easy to sharpen and cuts like a razor. Poor relief promises you only the fits. Even in the meat-packing industry, where people make their livings with knives, a common problem among professionals is improper relief on thin blades."

How far back should you taper a blade? The professional tapers his back, through trial and error, just short of the point where it will literally collapse with use. While the taxidermist need not be as concerned as a butcher, who uses his knife constantly for 8–10 hours a day, his knife should have and hold an edge better than most other knives, certainly better than a hunting knife or a knife used in the kitchen.

To get the proper relief, and ultimately a razor-sharp edge, Juranitch recommends the following procedure: To taper the blade back, use any handy coarse abrasive. A hone, the flat side of a grinding wheel (not on the machine), an abrasive cloth or disc, a piece of sanding belt, all will do the job. **Do not use a power device.** It's too dangerous. Place the blade almost flat against the abrasive of your choice and grind in a circular motion. Check the blade for "furrow marks"; these are the grind marks made by the abrasive. The farther up the blade these marks go, the better the end results. Grind until you can feel the burr along the entire length of the blade. A dry abrasive is used, no oil. Tests have proved that oil is not only messy and unnecessary, it gives an inferior edge. The grit extracted from the stone becomes suspended in the oil along with the metal filings from the blade; this creates a grinding compound, similar to the stuff used to grind the valves on a car. Running the blade through this compound is like running it through a pile of sand. The edge comes into direct contact with the abrasive, and the result is a poor edge.

Once you've developed a burr on each side of the blade, you can, using a finer abrasive, repeat the process and remove the coarse furrow marks from the sides of the blade. Juranitch advises against this, however, unless you are cutting something thick, such as cold fat.

"I have never seen anyone," he comments, "who could

sharpen a knife as good free-handed, and with the proper angle and control, as he can with a mechanical guide. Using the proper equipment for the first time, it's possible to create an edge far superior to that produced by the best professional using the free-hand method."

To prepare the edge, clamp the sharpening guide on the back of the blade *(illustration 17-2)*. After some preliminary grinding with a coarse abrasive to achieve the proper relief, switch to a fine hone. Place the guide on the hone first, then the edge. During the finishing stroke, the sharpening guide must remain in contact with the abrasive at all times to assure the proper angle. Lifting the guide while the edge stays in contact with the hone will ruin the edge.

With the guide and edge both in contact, draw the blade across the hone *in slow motion,* watching closely as the knife edge wipes the hone from the tip of the blade to the hilt. Alternate this procedure, turning the blade after each stroke, about 12 strikes total on either side. You should now have an edge that can easily shave hair off your arm.

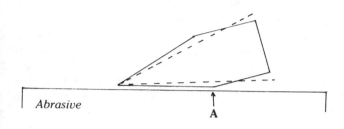

Abrasive

A

17-1. An example of a knife with poor relief.

17-2. A sharpening guide is clamped to the back of the blade.

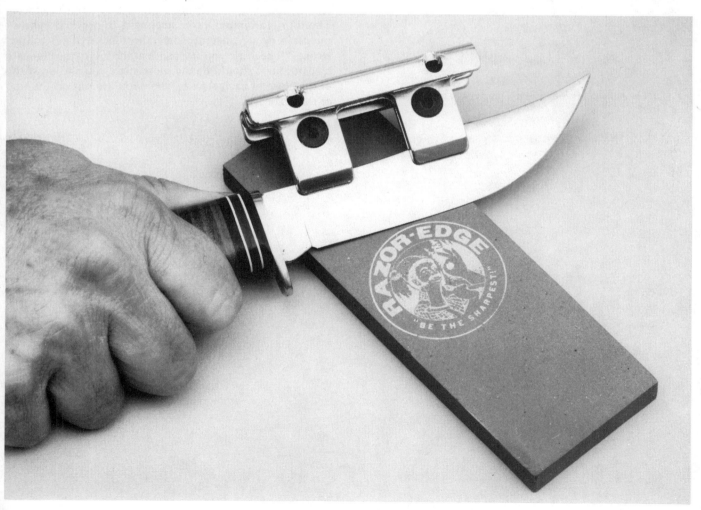

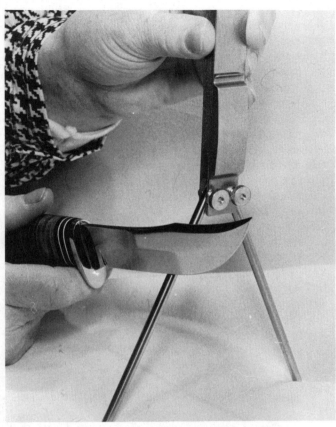

17-3. Once the edge has been properly prepared, it is finished on a steel.

Once the edge is prepared, finish it on a steel *(illustration 17-3)*.

The best way to test a knife edge is on a whole chicken. It has bones, skin, fat, cartilage—and it's cheap. Lightly and cautiously, cut away the skin, fat, and bone. Feel how the blade cuts. Now use a proper steel. A kitchen steel is acceptable if you have one, but the results may not be as satisfactory because of its rougher finish. A smooth steel is far superior. After steeling, try cutting with your knife again. You should note a big difference.

"Once you have a superb edge, use only the steel as you work," says Juranitch. "While a steel puts the finishing touch on the edge, it also maintains the sharpness of the edge as you use it. A good professional butcher with a production knife will use only the steel once his blade is prepared. He has no reason to return to the abrasive unless he damages the edge; and he should steel only when he feels it's necessary. The steel he uses should, moreover, be so smooth that the butcher can see his face in the reflection."

How he uses it is also important. According to Juranitch, the proper technique takes study and practice. The thing to remember in steeling is to proceed lightly, maintaining a constant angle throughout the steeling stroke. "The angle you start with at the hilt of the blade," he cautions, "should be the same angle you end up with at the close of each stroke, when you are out on the tip of the blade."

18/Dare to Be Different

18/Dare to Be Different

If you have read the preceding chapters, you should now have some understanding of basic taxidermy, but you can't fully appreciate what is involved until you start and finish a project.

One common problem should be considered before you begin your first taxidermy job. That is finding and maintaining adequate work space. If you have to put everything away after each step, then bring it all out and get organized again before you continue, you may soon become discouraged. Maybe you can "borrow" a portion of the garage until you are finished. If everything is laid out and ready to go, it is much easier to return to the project. If possible, plan to devote some time to the project each day; only in that way will you carry it to completion. Self-discipline is important to successful taxidermy.

If you get into taxidermy and like it, you undoubtedly will wonder about future opportunities, including the possibilities for making it a full-time profession. Or you might want to get into taxidermy as a sideline at home to supplement your regular income.

There is a future in taxidermy *if you are good enough*. That means more than simply turning out quality work, although you are doomed to failure unless you provide a professional product.

A taxidermist's best advertising is word of mouth.

When a customer recommends you to someone else, that is a compliment to be treasured. But a reputation has to be earned, time and again. Each mount you turn out should be the very best work you can do.

Keep in mind that when someone brings in a bird or fish or whatever to be mounted, he is pretty excited about the whole deal. He is eager to see the finished product. Still, he may not understand that quality taxidermy takes time, and if he doesn't, be sure to bring that fact to his attention. But if you promise the finished mount in 6 weeks, make every effort to have it ready on time. The customer will be greatly disappointed if you fail to keep your end of the bargain. That is not the way to get recommended to others.

You can learn much by visiting and watching professional taxidermists. Most are helpful if you are sincere and courteous with your requests. If you are seriously considering making this your profession, you might attempt to secure a part-time job with a local taxidermist. As I have mentioned, there is no substitute for practical experience. You do not become proficient in taxidermy overnight. You must work at it and continually try to improve.

There are certain mechanics of taxidermy to be mastered, including skill with your hands. But more important are individual and personal creativity and ingenuity. Each taxidermist "sees" and does things differently. In the same way, several painters may use the same basic methods to put colors on a canvas, but the finished products will be totally different. Each has his own conception of what he is painting.

The step-by-step procedures detailed in this book are the ones that a single taxidermist, Lem Rathbone, uses. To be sure, there are sometimes alternative methods in some instances. These happen to be the ones that Rathbone finds to be best to satisfy his own particular needs.

As you progress in taxidermy, you might not be totally satisfied with Rathbone's methods. Don't hesitate to pursue your own ideas. Dare to be different. You might come up with techniques that are better for what you are trying to achieve. In taxidermy there are certain fundamentals but they are not inflexible.

One hobby taxidermist, for example, utilizes balsawood bodies for his bird mounts. He cuts a block of balsa to the precise dimensions and shape required for the intended job. He says he has trouble wrapping excelsior tightly enough for a body; he likes the balsa wood much better.

You might try this, and if balsa wood isn't readily available, you can substitute Styrofoam, chunks of which can be bought at most department stores. If Styrofoam isn't available in the thickness needed, glue two or three pieces together. But remember to get a glue that is compatible with Styrofoam.

Another taxidermy hobbyist delights in chopping up a mannequin and putting it back together in the shape he desires. He attempts to make his mounts a bit different from others he has seen. He is continually experimenting, never satisfied with the ordinary. Each mount is an adventure of sorts.

But in the end, no matter what you do or how you do it, the mount should appear lifelike. If a mount doesn't look just right, study photographs of live animals (or birds or fish) and try to determine where you went wrong.

For this purpose, it pays to keep a file of clippings. The photographs of live animals and birds which illustrate chapter 2 of this book are examples. Such photographs give you an idea of how a creature really looks in life. Some magazines, such as *National Wildlife*, use numerous full-color illustrations of live specimens.

Get publications such as this, clip the illustrations, and put them in your file. With fish particularly, color illustrations are invaluable when you are attempting to paint a mount. Many books also feature illustrations of live creatures. Collect a modest reference library. Then, as you work on a mount, you can have a photograph handy to check details.

Finally, don't hesitate to use any commercial aids available. A mount built from scratch is not necessarily better or more satisfying than one for which you purchase some of the materials needed. In the long run, buying commercial products can be less expensive. Seldom can you make something cheaper that others mass-produce.

Mannequins are one example. If you only need one or two, it is much cheaper and simpler to order a mannequin from a taxidermy supply house and alter it to fit your individual needs than to buy everything needed to construct it. Hundreds of mannequins can be made from one mold, unless it gets damaged. It makes no sense to build a mold, use it once, and throw it away.

As another example, maybe you want to make a belt or hat band from a snake skin. Many ingredients go into the glycerin-base tanning solution. You can't buy these ingredients in small quantities, yet you need only a minuscule amount. Instead of hustling about in search of the glycerin and the various acids required, the economical approach is to purchase a 1-ounce bottle of the solution, sufficient for a typical snake skin, from a taxidermy supply house such as Austin Taxidermist (see appendix). Nail the skin, flesh side out, on a board and smear on the tanning solution. In less than a week the skin will be cured and ready to be converted into a belt or a hat band, according to its length.

In most instances you will come out ahead by buying necessary basic items rather than trying to improvise. There are exceptions, of course, such as making a bird or fish mannequin by shaping a chunk of inexpensive Styrofoam. You will find what you can or cannot do once you get involved in taxidermy.

It is best, however, to complete two or three beginner jobs before you get imaginative and begin to improvise and experiment. No matter what you are doing there are some fundamentals to be followed, certain steps to be completed in sequence. Ignore the fundamentals and you are asking for trouble.

19/Taxidermy Tips

19/Taxidermy Tips

Try to find a spot with adequate space not only to do the work but to leave everything spread out until you finish. It takes time and effort to remove everything then restore it between steps.

***

Taxidermy takes time. Be sure you budget sufficient time to complete what you start.

***

There are no magic shortcuts in taxidermy. Each step must be completed to the best of your ability before you progress to the next.

***

It is easy to forget something as you work, only to realize your oversight later, and by then it might be too late. For this reason, once you have read a chapter, make a systematic checklist of the successive steps and mark off each one as you finish it.

***

Check to make sure you have all the necessary tools and materials before you begin a job. This could save some headaches later.

***

If you are attempting to mount a big-game head and the cape is badly damaged, it is much easier and you'll have a better-quality job if you can obtain another cape and substitute it. If possible, get a cape of approximately the same size.

***

In restoring an old mount, if the mannequin still is good you need only to replace the aged cape with a fresh one. If the mannequin is bad, remove the skull plate with the antlers or horns and start from scratch.

***

If you find a pair of shed antlers you would like to mount, obtain a skull plate with antlers attached. Saw off the antlers flush against the skull. Obtain two two-way screws, pointed and threaded at both ends. With a drill slightly smaller than the screw, make a hole at each of the spots where you removed the antlers, and also into the base of each of the antlers that you plan to substitute for the ones you removed. Have the holes deep enough so that when you screw one end of a screw into the skull plate and the other into the base of the new antler, you can turn the antler until it is screwed firmly against the skull plate.

***

When making papier-mâché, if to each gallon of water you add 1 cup of vinegar you accomplish two goals: vinegar slows the setting process, and it also deodorizes the papier-mâché, giving it a cleaner smell.

***

One place to look for a perch on which to place a mounted bird is along a lake, a man-made impoundment or a stream. Driftwood comes in various shapes and sizes, and it is easy to find what you need.

***

If you mount a bird with an abundance of pinfeathers, although the mount will look good when first completed, the pinfeathers usually fall out within a year's time and the mount deteriorates.

***

After you have mounted two or three birds, you probably will want to get more professional about your work. One way to improve the quality of a mount is to wash the bird. (Museums require that all birds be washed.) Put a small amount of mild detergent into enough lukewarm water to cover the specimen. Wash it thoroughly, change the water, add more detergent and wash again. The skin must then be thoroughly rinsed in clean water, maybe changing the water once or twice, because the bird will not fluff dry if any soap remains in the feathers. Press the skin in your hands to remove as much water as possible. Now put the skin into borax and work it around to get the borax into every crease to preserve the skin. Don't worry about getting borax on the feathers; it will come off as the feathers dry. Hang the skin to dry in a cool spot (out of the sun) or in front of a fan. Periodically pick up the skin and shake it to fluff as it dries. Once dried, the feathers will be thicker and have a much better color.

***

While the art of taxidermy is old, there are recent innovations. One is a line of mannequins from Jonas

Brothers, Inc., of Denver, Colorado, called Flexiforms *(illustration 19-1)*. Available for both birds and animals, Flexiforms are made from a soft rubberlike substance and you can twist the head and bend the legs to achieve any shape you desire. The only drawback is that such mannequins are rather expensive, even for small animals and birds. Also from Jonas Brothers is a line of big-game head mannequins molded from a plasticlike material that is both strong and lightweight. The biggest improvement of this mannequin over a handmade one is that the eyes, nose and lips have perfect detail.

***

Be very careful with the equipment you use, especially sharp instruments. A common mistake is to stick the point of a knife into the table as you work. The chances are good that you will reach for something without looking, run your hand against the exposed knife blade and suffer a nasty cut.

***

The most common mistake when painting a fish is to apply paint or lacquer too thick. Many light coats of very thin paint or lacquer (never mix the two) are much better than one thick coat, which tends to obscure all detail.

***

If you have a mold and you want to make a cast, first wet the mold thoroughly and leave a little excess water inside. As you pour plaster into the mold, it will force water to the surface, eliminating any air. If you attempt to cast in a dry mold, you invariably get some air bubbles.

***

When you are attempting to model a snake into a particular shape in order to freeze it and make a mold later, you may have trouble getting the reptile to stay in the position you want. Shape it the best you can, place it in the freezer and check on it periodically. As the snake begins to freeze and gets firm but not yet hard, remove it from the freezer, adjust the position to the shape you desire, then put it back to finish freezing.

***

When attempting to tan a hide for the first time, select a small animal. The size and texture of the hide make it easier and quicker to tan. One of the best-quality hides for tanning is that from a common house cat. To get a specimen, contact a veterinarian. Vets often get stray or injured cats which must be put to sleep and usually the dead animals go unclaimed.

***

Always use a sharp knife. A dull blade does an inferior job and is much more difficult to work with.

***

Always work with inflammable materials in a well-

ventilated area, preferably outdoors. No-lead gasoline is very hazardous.

***

After working with borax and other chemicals, wash your hands thoroughly with soap. Otherwise, if you handle food, and take any chemicals internally, they could make you sick.

***

Keep tools and working area clean. Metals such as

19-1. This is a Flexiform mannequin of a ground squirrel. The neck and legs can easily be bent to any shape you desire.

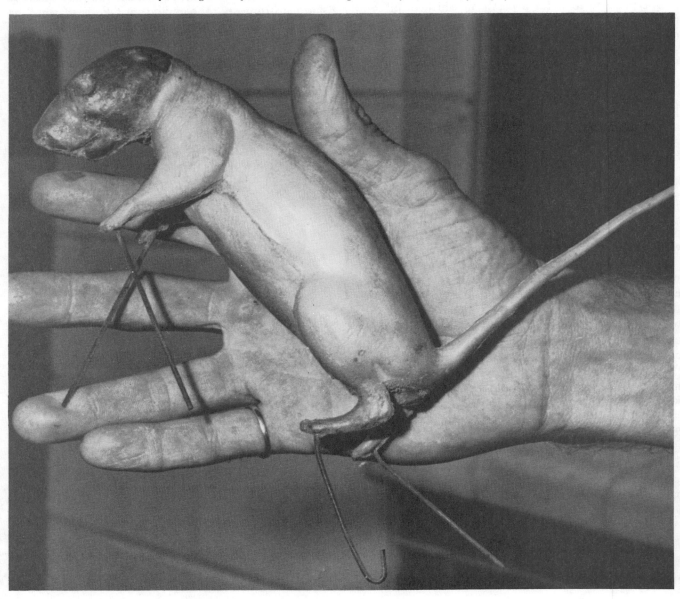

knife blade, hammer heads and pliers should be sprayed with WD-40 or oiled lightly. Working around salt will cause tools to rust overnight.

***

Safety goggles should be worn when working with power tools such as a band saw or sander.

***

Wear rubber gloves when handling and mixing chemicals. You may be allergic to certain substances.

***

Have your work area adequately lighted. You will do a better job in good light.

***

Store chemicals in sealed containers in a dry place. Plaster will absorb moisture and become lumpy and useless. But do not store any inflammable materials. Buy sufficient amounts only as you need them.

***

If mixed fire clay or potter's clay is not to be used immediately, wrap in a moist (not wet) cloth to prevent drying and hardening.

***

Do not paint with lacquer when humidity is high. As the lacquer dries, it will absorb moisture and turn a milky white.

***

Watch for parasites on mounted specimens. Pests can ruin a mount. Spray lightly with a bug killer such as Real Kill.

***

Do not shellac or lacquer antlers or horns. Instead, use boiled linseed oil to restore the natural dark color.

Older mounts particularly need a linseed oil application. After the oil is applied, immediately wipe off any that the horns or antlers do not absorb. Linseed oil also can be used on plaques and shields.

***

Store mannequins made of papier-mâché and glue in a dry place until needed for mounting. Keep foam-rubber and plastic mannequins away from excessive heat, or they will melt.

***

Do not handle hides or skins excessively with hands except while doing the mounting job. Body temperature has been known to make animal hair, bird feathers and fish scales loosen and fall out.

***

For tedious cutting jobs, a scalpel is more efficient than a knife. Most taxidermy supply houses (see Appendix) sell scalpels.

***

To obtain a particular mannequin (form) in a hurry, check first with a local taxidermist; he may just have what you need on hand.

***

If you don't own a spray gun, and you need only a small amount of lacquer, try shopping at an auto-parts store. You'll find lacquers of different colors in spray cans are readily available.

***

Most taxidermy supply houses stock a complete line of water-based, nontoxic colors for painting fish.

***

Instead of trying to make your own papier-mache, order it in dry bulk from a taxidermy supply house. Mix only enough for your purposes.

Appendix

Appendix

GLASS EYE REFERENCE CHART

Glass eyes can be obtained from a local taxidermist or a taxidermy supply company; the latter can provide information on eye sizes for protected birds.

BIRDS

Crow	9 mm, black
Coot	8 mm, red
Canary	3 mm, brown
Grouse	9 mm, brown
Snow goose	11 mm, brown
Pheasant, male	10 and 11 mm, red with yellow ring
Pheasant, female	10 and 11 mm, brown
Pigeon	7 mm, red
Quail	6 mm, brown
Jack snipe	7 mm, brown
English sparrow	4 mm, brown
Turkey	13 mm, brown
Woodcock	10 mm, brown
Mourning dove	7 mm, brown

DUCKS

American golden eye	9 mm, yellow
American merganser	11 mm, red
Canvasback	10 mm, brown
Mallard	10 mm, brown
Teal	8 mm, brown
Wood duck, male	10 mm, red
Wood duck, female	10 mm, yellow
Bufflehead	10 mm, brown
Baldpate	10 mm, brown
Gadwall	11 mm, brown
Hooded merganser	11 mm, red
Pintail	9 mm, brown
Redhead	10 mm, yellow
Scaup	11 mm, yellow
Spoonbill	10 mm, yellow
Shoveler	10 mm, yellow
Harlequin	10 mm, brown
Ruddy	11 mm, hazel

DEER

Whitetail	24-28 mm
Mule deer	26-30 mm
Fawn	20 mm
Blacktail	26-28 mm
Elk	30-33 mm

OTHERS

Black bear	14-16 mm
Bobcat	16-18 mm
Caribou	26-29 mm
Cottontail rabbit	13 mm
Jack rabbit	16 mm
Gray fox	14 mm
Red fox	15 mm
Antelope	26-29 mm
Beaver	12 mm
Badger	10 mm
Coyote	16 mm
Chipmunk	5 mm
Mountain goat	20-25 mm
Mountain sheep	26-29 mm
Mink	8 mm
Muskrat	7 mm
Opossum	9 mm
Otter	12 mm
Javelina (peccary)	16 mm
Porcupine	10 mm
Raccoon	12 mm
Skunk	8 mm
Squirrel	10-11 mm
Lynx	18-20 mm
Wolverine	13-14 mm

SUPPLY SOURCES

(When ordering, write the supply house of your choice and ask if there's a charge for their catalog. Include a self-addressed, stamped envelope).

Austin Taxidermist Studio
8739 Highway 290W
Austin, Texas 78736

Dan Chase Taxidermy Supply Co.
13599 Blackwater Road
Baker, Louisiana 70714

Elwood Co.
Omaha, Nebraska 68102

Jonas Brothers, Inc.
1901 S. Bannock St.
Denver, Colorado 80223

McKenzie Taxidermy Supply
P.O. Box 480
Granite Quarry
North Carolina 28072

Razor Edge Systems, Inc.
P.O. Box 150
Ely, Minnesota 55731
(Knife sharpening supplies)

Van Dykes
Woonsocket, South Dakota 57385

WCW Mesquite Co.
Hondo, Texas 78661
(Panels and plaques)

TAXIDERMY MAGAZINES

Breakthrough
P.O. Box 967
Monroe, Georgia 30655

Taxidermy Today
119 Gadsen Street
Chester, South Carolina 29706

TAXIDERMY CORRESPONDENCE COURSES

Northwestern School of Taxidermy
P.O. Box 3507
Omaha, Nebraska 68103

American Wildlife Studios
P.O. Box 16030
Baton Rouge, Louisiana 70803

Taxidermy Supply Company
P.O. Box 5815-T
Bossier City, Louisiana 71010

FORMULAS

DRY PRESERVE

To make a small amount of quick preserve, mix thoroughly 3 parts Borax with 1 part baking soda (to eliminate odor).

PAPIER-MÂCHÉ
(General use)

Ingredients needed: paper pulp, powdered dextrin, phenol, plaster of Paris.

Soak ordinary newspapers in water for two or three days, then work the saturated paper with your hands until you get pulp. Add an equal amount of powdered dextrin. Dextrin is a carbohydrate found in the sap of plants that has an adhesive quality. It can be ordered from a taxidermy supply house. Let the mixture soak for several hours or until the dextrin completely dissolves. Add 1 teaspoon phenol (available from drugstores). This can be put in a sealed container and kept indefinitely.

Part of the papier-mâché can be removed in the amount you need. Mix this with an equal amount of plaster of Paris. Upon drying it is bone hard.

Commercial papier-mâché: Available from taxidermy supply houses. Add water.

PAPIER-MÂCHÉ AND GLUE

4 parts papier-mâché (by weight)
1 part yellow dextrin glue

Prepare papier-mâché as explained in the preceding formula. Add the glue and mix thoroughly. Use fairly promptly, since once the mixture dries it becomes very hard and is permanent. It is good for such jobs as increasing the size of a mannequin in places where needed. When the hide is put back on, the mixture will not absorb water and soften, as will general-use papier-mâché

YELLOW DEXTRIN GLUE
(For making mannequins)
1 5-pound sack flour
2 pounds dextrin
3 gallons boiling water

Thoroughly mix the flour and dextrin. Add the boiling water. Pour the mixture back and forth from one container to another until it thickens. If it is too thin, add more flour; if too thick, add more boiling water.

PICKLING SOLUTION
(General use)
4 gallons water
8 pounds salt
1 pound alum
1 pound 20 Mule Team Borax

Bring the water to a boil, add the three dry ingredients, and stir until the powders are completely dissolved. Allow the pickle to cool completely before using.

PICKLING SOLUTION
(To preserve velveted antlers to prevent the velvet from ruining)

Mix 3 parts of 6-percent formaldehyde solution (available at drugstores) with 97 parts of water. Submerge the velvet-covered antlers in this and leave for a week to 10 days.

MOLD SEPARATOR A
(For making casts)
1 part petroleum jelly
1 part turpentine
1 part beeswax

Mix the ingredients thoroughly and keep in a sealed jar.

MOLD SEPARATOR B
1 part stearic acid
1 part kerosene

Mix the two liquids and keep in a sealed container.

FINISHING WAX
(For use around eyes and mouth of big-game mounts, fish, etc.)
8 ounces paraffin
8 ounces beeswax
1 ounce resin
2 drams turpentine

If the wax is too heavy, add more turpentine; should it be too light, add more beeswax.

STAIN TO RESTORE COLOR
OF BLEACHED ANTLERS

Dissolve a teaspoon of potassium permanganate (available from drugstores) in one-half cup of warm water. Mix and test on a small part of the antler. If the solution is too dark, add more water; should it be too light, put in a few more drops of potassium permanganate.

BACKING FOR FINS AND TAIL OF FISH
(Added to back of fins and tail for support)

9 parts powdered hide glue (available from taxidermy
  supply houses and most lumber yards).
1 part glycerine
Sufficient water to obtain the consistency desired.

Mix the ingredients and warm the substance in a dou-
ble boiler before using; it is rubbery when cool. Paint on
the backside of fins and tail.

Tanning Formulas

BASIC TANNING
(Hair On)

FORMULA A

1 pound alum
2 pounds salt
4 gallons water (soft water, if possible)

Mix the ingredients, stirring until the chemicals are
completely dissolved. Use in plastic container; chemicals
will corrode metal. Shaved hide must be submerged in
this solution at least a week or more before final hand-
finishing.

FORMULA B

2 pounds iron-free aluminum sulfate
2 pounds salt
6 ounces gambier or terra japonica
Stir aluminum sulfate and salt together in 2 gallons of
warm, soft water in a plastic container until chemicals

are dissolved. In a separate container dissolve the gambier or terra japonica in 2 quarts of water. Then mix the
two liquids thoroughly and add enough water to make 4
gallons of solution.

BUCKSKIN
(Hair Off)
*(To be used prior to use of either of the two preceding for-
mulas (see chapter 13, Tanning)*

1 pound hydrated lime (highly toxic)
4 ounces boric acid
Mix the hydrated lime in 1 gallon of warm water, using a plastic container. Then add water to have 4 gallons
of solution. Soak hide in this for a week or more, or until the hair comes off easily. Once the hair is completely
removed, mix the boric acid in 4 gallons of water and
submerge hide in this to neutralize any remaining lime.

SNAKESKIN TAN

Because of the many ingredients needed and the small
amount required to tan a snakeskin, you will save
money by purchasing the prepared solution (see Austin
Taxidermist, in Appendix). Only about 2 ounces are
needed for a large snakeskin. This is effective on any
American snake. After snake is skinned, tack hide on
board, flesh side out, and paint on the solution. Its glycerin base will make the skin pliable. Put the skin in a dry,
cool spot and leave it a week or more, or until the skin
is completely dried. It can then be used to make such
novelties as belts or hat bands.

A Gallery of Typical Mounts

Dall sheep.

Mule deer.

Blackbuck antelope.

Pronghorn antelope.

Head mount of a bobcat.

Head mount of a gray fox.

Ringtail cat.

A Mouflon sheep.

Typical whitetail deer.

Hawk in an open-wing mount.

Sparrow hawk.

Ringneck pheasant.

Hooded merganser duck (female).

Bluejay in an upright position.

Bluejay in a more active pose.

Closed-wing mount of a hawk.

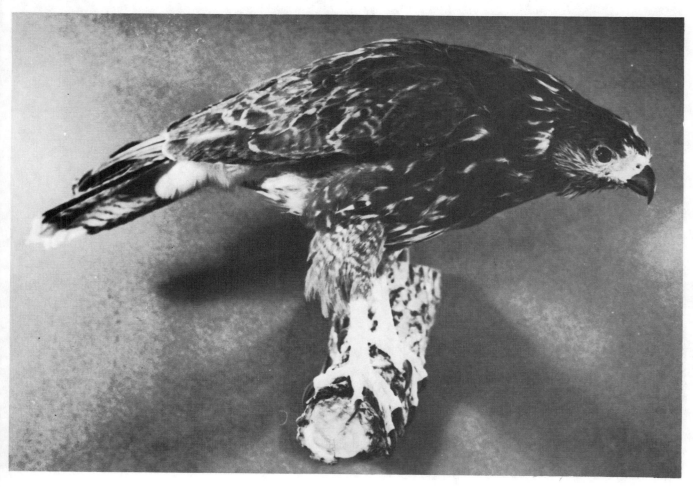

Freshly painted largemouth black bass hung to dry.

Index
(Page numbers in boldface refer to illustrations.)